Arcadia Borealis

To my daughters
Genevieve and Olivia
—when they are *much* older

Arcadia Borealis

Childhood and Youth in Northern Ontario

by
George Case

Your Scrivener Press

Copyright © 2008 George Case

No part of this book may be reproduced or transmitted in any form by any means, except for brief passages quoted by a reviewer, without written permission from the publisher—or, in the case of photocopying, a license from Access ©: the Canadian Copyright Licensing Agency.

Library and Archives Canada Cataloguing in Publication

Case, George, 1967-
　　Arcadia borealis : childhood and youth in northern Ontario / by George Case.

ISBN 978-1-896350-27-1

　　1. Case, George, 1967- --Childhood and youth. 2. Ontario, Northern--Biography. I. Title.
FC3094.25.C38A3 2008　　971.3'1　　C2008-901324-7

Book design: Laurence Steven
Cover design: Chris Evans
Cover photos of author: courtesy of George Case
Cover painting: Franz Johnston, "The Fire Ranger," 1921
　　—photo © National Gallery of Canada; —National Gallery of Canada, Ottawa

Published by *Your Scrivener Press*
465 Loach's Road,
Sudbury, Ontario, Canada, P3E 2R2
info@yourscrivenerpress.com
www.yourscrivenerpress.com

We acknowledge the support of the Canada Council for the Arts and the Ontario Arts Council for their support of our publishing program.

 Canada Council　Conseil des Arts
for the Arts　　　du Canada
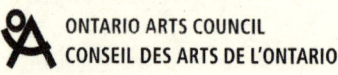

Notes and Acknowledgements

Other than those of public figures like politicians, artists, and entertainers, all names in these pieces have been changed to protect the innocent.

The title "Arcadia Borealis" was conceived without knowledge of the Nobel prize-winning Swedish poet Erik Axel Karlfeldt's poetry collection of the same name; this work has no connection to his.

Thanks to T-Rex and Essex Music for permission to quote a selection from "Raw Ramp":

Words and Music by Marc Bolan © Copyright 1971 (Renewed) Onward Music Ltd., London, England. TRO-Essex Music International, Inc., New York, controls all publication rights for the U.S.A. and Canada. Used by permission.

Contents

Terre Sauvage
    The Solemn Land   11
    Street of Dreams   19
    In Search Engines of Lost Time   27
    Satan & Me   35
    Pikangikum   43
    The Most Perfect Moment   49

Fire-Swept, Algoma
    Mine   57
    The Four Freaks   65

The West Wind
    Victim of Changes   131
    Sad Wings of Destiny   137
    Arcadia Borealis   149
    The Return of the Native   157

About the Author   171

There's not a joy the world can give like that it takes away,
When the glow of early thought declines in feeling's dull decay;
'Tis not on youth's smooth cheek the blush alone, which fades so fast,
But the tender bloom of heart is gone, ere youth itself be past.
— George Gordon, Lord Byron, "There's Not a Joy"

There was nothing but the pine plain ahead of him, until the far blue hills that marked the Lake Superior height of land. He could hardly see them, faint and far away in the heat-light over the plain. If he looked too steadily they were gone. But if he only half-looked they were there, the far-off hills of the height of land.
— Ernest Hemingway, "Big Two-Hearted River"

Part I

Terre Sauvage

The Solemn Land

MY FRIEND CHRIS was once riding a Greyhound bus from Toronto north back home to Sault Ste. Marie and found himself seated beside a traveller from Germany. After exchanging pleasantries with the guy Chris nodded off, until he started awake a few hours later to find his fellow passenger excitedly looking out the windows and snapping pictures. Puzzled, Chris looked around for whatever had caught the Teutonic tourist's eye—he didn't see anything. Why the sudden interest? "There is *nothing here*," said the seatmate, delighted. "There are only trees! There are no people or houses or anything!" The central European was experiencing the North American hinterland for the first time, countless generations of village and town and city speeding headlong into a planetary tract of forest and trying to comprehend. "Yeah, well, get used to it," Chris told him with a shrug, and went back to sleep. They were just south of Parry Sound, he reckoned.

It is indeed difficult for urbanites—and most of us are,

nowadays—to grasp the sheer immeasurable space of a country like Canada and a region like northern Ontario. Distances get distorted between a local transit guide and a trucker's highway atlas; what might be a two- or three-hour trek from one end of the city limits to another would be a short hop by float plane in the bush, and a dizzying city circuit from Chinatown to Little Italy past Skid Row and towards the gentrified waterfront might get you a quarter way around some nameless lake in the middle of nowhere. Cities are dots on the map, but the great wide open *is* the map. In 1906 the English occultist Aleister Crowley journeyed by train from Vancouver east across the new dominion, and even the legendary magician was shaken by the immensities of scale nature revealed to him: "As for the ghastly monotony of wilderness... through Calgary and Winnipeg on to Toronto—words fortunately fail... Of all the lifeless, loveless lands that writhe beneath the wrath of God, commend me to Canada!"

Northern Ontario is both a political sub-unit defined by cartography and public administration, and a physical phenomenon comprising the geologies and botanies of Lakes Superior and Huron, the Canadian Shield or Laurentian Plateau, the boreal forest of mixed deciduous giving way to increasingly uniform coniferous woods, and an incalculable network of small lakes and rivers chipped out of the earth during the last ice age. Historically it is Canada's first frontier (predating the nation's legal inauguration by two hundred years), the route of trappers and missionaries and fur-trading *voyageurs*, an awesome evergreen obstacle of blackflies and desolation and cold before the breadbasket of the great temperate grasslands opened out. Culturally, it is not the far north of Pierre Berton, Farley Mowat, or Ted Harrison, nor is it the prairies of W.O. Mitchell or William Kurelek, or the British Columbia of Emily Carr or Pauline Johnson, or the sophisticated cosmopolitan centres of Mordecai Richler, Glenn Gould, Leonard Cohen or Douglas Coupland. It is the Canada of Grey Owl's Lake Temagami and Norval Morriseau's shaman shapeshifters; it is the Gitchee Gumee of Gordon Lightfoot's "The Wreck of the Edmund Fitzgerald," the Inco mines of Stompin' Tom Connors' "Sudbury Saturday Night," and the Blind River of Neil Young's "Long May You Run." It is the "vast area of deeply wooded wilderness...a country of far-flung, lonely farms and a few widely scattered small towns and villages" of Sheila Burnford's *The Incredible Journey*, where "human beings together are as a handful of sand upon the ocean shores, and for the most part there is silence and solitude." It is the Highway 17 of Terry Fox, hobbling to his final, fatal, rendezvous with cancer just before Thunder Bay, a few weeks after my father and I saw him outside Desbarats, staring straight through his pain while we and the other bystanders cheered him into town.

It is a land of short summers and long winters, famous for the colours of its autumns—the Algoma Central Railway carries eager sightseers into the red, orange and yellow Agawa Canyon every fall—and less known for the ubiquitous annoyance of thawing dog shit universally cursed every spring. Wildlife is common in the territory, either as sportsmen's trophies, or roadkill, or unremarkable outdoor encounters. It is not unusual to hear of bears or deer or moose spotted within city limits or even, disoriented and alone, wandering around downtown of a predawn summer morning. The exoticism such animals hold for metropolitans is lost on the farmers, campers, drivers, and hunters who live and work among them. I can remember Sault Ste. Marie being reblanketed by a blizzard in May, and a January power failure that shut down the streetlights in the middle of the night: such was the whiteness and volume of the snow that its reflected light made 2:00 a.m. appear as some fantastically overcast midday. I remember the whole-body tension of walking outside in winter, the sub-zero taut tightening of the innards that would not relax until a few minutes after coming in again. June and July are precious flourishes of heat and growth and life, warned by August, scolded by September, shut down by Thanksgiving and ruled out by Christmas. December is greeting-card picturesque: red, blue and green lights twinkling over the icicles and ski trails and outdoor skating rinks; the colours are turned off through January, February, March and April while the icicles remain.

Sault Ste. Marie is called "the hub of the Great Lakes," and on maps appeared to my childish imagination as the wrung neck of a grossly ballooned horse, with Lake Superior as the head, Lake Michigan as the front legs and Lake Huron the hindquarters. In reality its near enclosure by water in an otherwise landlocked part of the world made for curiously maritime weather patterns, hence all that snow for one-third of each year. The greatness of the lakes was visible to a spectator as one of the waterway's thousand-foot freighters navigated up Lake Huron's North Channel into the Saint Mary's River: first the bridge emerged, then the bow, then the massive elongated hull, and finally the stern and its identifying insignia painted on its smokestack. Thousands of miles from any ocean, the curvature of the earth could be observed in Sault Ste. Marie, Ontario.

People of the area acquire a detachment from the newer,

faster, bigger life to the south. As Canada in the later decades of the twentieth century ran to embrace a post-industrial, multicultural identity, the pulp mills and Kiwanis clubs of northern Ontario came to seem like vague embarrassments. Canadians were told by the likes of Pierre Trudeau and Marshall McLuhan that they were no longer the proverbial hewers of wood and drawers of water—the wood-hewing, water-drawing folk living off the lands around Lake Superior, and the hockey players and steelworkers and fishing guides, could be forgiven for feeling like exiles in their own country. The telecommunications boom of the 1970s onward brought often incongruous sounds and pictures from far away; I recall watching other kids in my high school adopt Mohawk haircuts and ghetto moves, and thinking that while punk rock and breakdancing might be authentic styles in London or New York or Los Angeles, or even Toronto, they looked awfully affected in Sault Ste. Marie. Northern Ontario's geography—its pre-Cambrian permanence and its inexorable solstitial rhythms—is a constant rebuke to the ephemeral whims and fancies of human conceit. Only the native Ojibway could claim to be above such follies, those of their white neighbours no less than the Yonge Street hipster's—for years a train bridge by the Garden River Indian Reserve conveyed a solemn graffito to motorists on the Trans-Canada highway: "THIS IS INDIAN LAND / INDIAN POWER / We will WIN." The Ojibway had never been exiled. "Sure, we'll give them back their land," I used to hear in reply, after the last empty went into the case, "if they give *us* back liquor and the wheel." This was the original social dynamic acted out upon the scarred surface of the Laurentian Plateau.

I am a third-generation northern Ontarian. My paternal

grandmother was from the railroad stop of Massey, on Lake Huron's north shore, and was in the first graduating class of Sault Ste. Marie's first high school, in 1917. Her oldest son, my father, was born in the silver town of Cobalt and lived there from 1929 to 1937. My mother was born in Ottawa in 1927 but grew up in a gold rush outpost called Red Lake, near the Manitoba border, where her entrepreneur father ran a sawmill and, later, a general store. For these and other reasons my notion of the Canadian character is based not on free health care or the CBC, but on the indescribable thick green smell of pine and birch woods and their carpets of moss and leaves and needles, on paddling a kayak on Batchawana Bay at my mother's beach house on Lake Superior, on tapping and boiling maple syrup at my father's cabin behind Echo Bay. I don't need tourist brochures or beer advertisements or the government to confirm who I am and where I am from. Grandparents, parents, and twenty years living underneath the cold, clear skies of northern Ontario told me what I needed to know.

Twenty years was all I had. I have lived away from the north for a long time, and I do not pretend to be a lifelong or unreconstructed Algoman. Since 1994 I have made my home in British Columbia's Lower Mainland: the epicentre of Canada's Pacific province, a famous, fast-growing port metropolis, built on a rain forest, crowded with all walks of life and all the virtues and vices of the wired, postmodern city state. Cutting-edge culture; irreversible Asian influence; birthplace of my daughters. Before that I lived five years in Ottawa: the nation's genteel capital, faux-Britannic grandeur and bureaucratic self-importance conjured up out of a Victorian lumber landing, daytimes of civil service pretensions blending into nights of underworld iniquity as fluently as Anglo accents blended into Québécois *joual*. Beer in quart bottles; late lenient hours; high highs and low lows. Before that it was two years in Toronto: a humid concrete jungle of ambition and vanity, Canada's twenty-four-hour Gotham on a flat, bland lakeshore conurbation. Scarce green space; riding all the way down the Bloor line at 6:30 AM; getting nowhere. Then there are my travels. Following fab footsteps across London's Abbey Road, treading the lunar heights of Alberta's Athabasca glacier. Las Vegas, Nevada—everything wrong with America and everything right, in one multibillion-dollar strip of materialism and reward. Finale Ligure, Italy—hostelling on the Riveria, my acoustic guitar echoing in the tiled hallways of an old monastery. Bruges, Belgium—reciting "In Flanders Fields" to a tour group on the spot where the trench poem was composed, picking World War I shrapnel out of the wet soil seventy years gone. Paros, Greece—the sun setting in the Cyclades, thinking of Matthew Arnold's melancholy "Dover Beach": "*Sophocles long ago / Heard it on the Aegean…*" That was at the far end of the Mediterranean Sea, where Sault Ste. Marie was on the other side of the world.

But northern Ontario is still there, even if I am not. In a digital future of megacities and fuel cells and expressways, that part of the province may depopulate altogether, the final remaining hewers of wood and drawers of water giving up and moving down to some beeping, flickering grid within the Windsor-Hamilton-Toronto-Ottawa-Montreal-Quebec corridor, or to Calgary-Edmonton or Vancouver-Seattle, and the lakes and trees and rocks will be left alone again, with no remembrance of their brief occupancy by human beings after the last ice age. There will be no more

Greyhound drivers absently listing off the scattered communities down the milk run from Sudbury to Sault Ste. Marie: "Now departing for Espanola, Serpent River, Iron Bridge, Bruce Mines..." There will be no more thousand-footers hauling iron ore east from Minnesota or grain south from the Lakehead through the St. Mary's River, no more Edmund Fitzgeralds and no more Terry Foxes. There will be no more outsiders to marvel at the range of green or height of blue, the depth of temperature or duration of winter, and no more resident northern Ontarians to take pride in such wonders as birthrights, the way I still do. Highway 17 might remain, slowly wearing down and mossing over, visible from space between the black water and the dark forest, like a signal from the lost civilization that once clustered thinly along it.

Street of Dreams

―――――

WHETHER WE ARE aware of it or not, most of us carry around an idea of "normalcy" established early in our lives. This day-to-day sense of what the world truly is or should be may have been completely suppressed or refuted by later experience, but deep down we each have a kind of inner origin myth, a pre-conscious understanding of our identity and our reality that has stayed with us in the same way the rituals and superstitions of ancient peoples have lingered on into post-industrial societies of the present.

My private origin myth became established between 1967 and 1975, when I lived on Lynn Road, in Sault Ste. Marie. Hardly more than a stunted offshoot of Wellington Street—it was a dead end that had exactly three houses on just one side—the first eight years of my existence passed there, and my earliest routines and expectations arose during this residency. Thus the only real homes for me are three-storey brick and have front porches, the only playgrounds for children are front sidewalks, back lanes, and parking lots, the only playmates are neighbour kids and the only Sunday dinner is roast beef and potatoes, followed by ice cream with chocolate sauce and then *The Wonderful World of Disney* and *The Beachcombers*. Memories other than these are deviations: maybe better, maybe worse, but still deviations. I have done a lot of branching off over the years, but I remember my roots.

Sault Ste. Marie stands at the foot of the Canadian Shield close by Lake Superior, a place of high wide horizons that rise over prehistoric rock to the north, inland seas to the west and the east, and the broad American heartland to the south, a kind of land's end in the middle of a continent. Lynn Road was just off Sault Ste. Marie's downtown core, within easy walking distance of an ordinary family's staple institutions circa 1972: Central Public School, Lakeway Collegiate and Vocational School, Sault Collegiate Institute High School, Dominion grocery store, St. Luke's Anglican cathedral, the Canadian Imperial Bank of Commerce, the Windsor coffee shop, the Orpheum and Odeon movie theatres, the post office, the courthouse, the public library, Jupiter variety store (with lunch counter), Sault Stationers, the smoke shop (the smoke shop!), the Liquor Control Board of Ontario, and Arthur Funeral Home. It might have been a toy village for some giant child, laid out as a perfect microcosm of everyday activity—work, school, commerce, justice, learning, recreation, worship, childhood, youth, adulthood, death.

This was no picket-fence suburbia. Behind our house was the train yard of the Canadian Pacific Railway, an expanse of gravel and scrap metal and rail lines we just called "the CPR." I didn't grow up on the wrong side of the tracks—I grew up right on them. At night we could hear the shunting of boxcars, flatcars, tankers, hoppers and engines, a thunderous steel rumble that seemed like a living, natural sound we barely noticed. A leafy, unpaved back laneway ran westward behind the houses of Wellington Street, and to the north was the Olympus of Collegiate Hill, looking down upon much of the city. There was a thin line of bush between our backyards and the CPR, including a secluded little clearing frequented by the more wretched denizens of Sault Ste. Marie's downtown that the neighbourhood children called, accurately, "Drunks' Hideout." The funeral home's parking lot stood at the end of Lynn Road and served as sporting field, battleground, movie set, racing track, and *terra nullius* for us kids; in the winter municipal ploughs and trucks piled snow at either end of the lot, recreating Gothic mountains and cliffs and castles in child's scales. By spring the snow turned into oceanic puddles and then dried up by summer, as another cycle of exploration, imagination, alliance and warfare began.

Because the road was so short and our parent-imposed boundaries so fixed by the train lines and the busier adjacent streets, we children lived in a self-contained conceptual nation I dreamed of as "Lynnwood." We devised flags, festivals, elections, rivalries, expeditions and armed forces that the grownups only noticed as playing or fighting, rather like a grittier, real-life version of the *Peanuts* or *Our Gang* universes. Over the course of a few months it was as if I had experienced my own Golden Age of Hollywood (elaborate variations of "Guns," "Cops & Robbers," and re-enactments of current movies like *The Towering Inferno* and *Airport '75*), World War II (stone- and water-balloon-throwing blitzkriegs across the front yards), and hunt for Bigfoot (stalking the elusive drunks in their wilderness lair). When

Charlie and I tried to achieve flight running at top speed while holding a plank of wood for a wing we were the Wright Brothers, when Kimmy was captured in battle and tied up with her skipping rope by Clinton and Paul she was Helen of Troy, a screeching car accident outside of March Street Confectionery was our *Titanic* disaster, and when a little dog was run over and killed instantly on Wellington Street as David and I watched, sitting on the lawn of Arthur Funeral Home, it was my first real encounter with sudden violent mortality. I am a proud Canadian, but I was a Lynnwood nationalist.

Things were different in the late 60s and early 70s. Depending on your historical perspective you can see the period as a distant precursor to our own twenty-first century culture—the United States mired in a controversial war, widespread anxiety over pollution and finite resources, restless youth with their drugs and scandalous pop music, the first hints that computers and television and other communications technologies would gradually be reshaping our collective psyches—or you might think, as I tend to, that those times were a last flourish of small-town, middle-class order and decorum, much more like 1950 or even 1920 than the early 2000s. I can remember watching my father select his stock of spirits from the lists posted up at the LCBO, and then a uniformed clerk would wrap up his picks in brown paper and hand the bottles over the counter to him. My mother knew the checkout girls at Dominion by name, and there she would give me a lone penny—all I needed—to buy gumballs from the store's vending machine. I can remember daily grocery delivery and little signs in front windows, "No Milk Today." Even around clanking train tracks and homeless alcoholics, parents were assured of their children's unsupervised safety. At Central the pupils were segregated by a boys' side and a girls' side at recess. My sister would walk over to March Street once a week and return with a paper bag of gumdrops she'd purchased for ten cents; packs of hockey cards were the same price (how exciting to find Bobby Orr once!). I can remember the entire audience standing for "O Canada" before the showing of a film. People seem to have been more literate, with newspapers and advertisements and public notices carrying more text and fewer graphics—nothing was wired, or digital, or cyber. After much pestering on my part, colour and cable TV (totalling ten or eleven channels) arrived in our house when I was about seven, bringing my favourite shows like *Bugs Bunny*, *Scooby-Doo*, *Charlie Brown* specials, and grown-up fare like *Mary Tyler Moore*, *Bob Newhart*, *All in the Family*, and *M*A*S*H*, as well as Canadian content like *Front Page Challenge*, *This is the Law*, and *Wayne & Schuster*. I have retained faint impressions of Vietnam, the energy crisis, the final moon landings, Watergate, and the breakup of the Beatles. Bruce Lee and Evel Knievel were Lynnwood's twin deities. Taking a long view, this is all quite recent news and culture, but for me it is literally a lifetime ago.

It is a cliché to point out that things have gone downhill since the old days, and it is a cliché to point out that it is a cliché: there's even a book by Arthur Herman called *The Idea of Decline in Western History*, suggesting that from Plato to Spengler, someone has always been lamenting how far we've fallen since the golden past. *La plus ça change*, et cetera. The moment in which I lived on Lynn Road has—again, depending on your perspective—either gone from an age of public virtues, shared social welfare and a thriving democracy to one of rampant privatization, corporatization, and a widening income gap, or from an era of sturdy Anglo-Judeo-Christian obligations and a pervasive sense of civic cohesion to one based on entitlement, self, and a relativist disdain for standards, achievement, or sacrifice. Perhaps Lynn Road was a watershed, with "O Canada," *Front Page Challenge*, and the Windsor coffee shop on one side, and cell phones, *American Idol*, and Starbucks on the other.

Or maybe it's just me. Years later, as a young man, I was living in Ottawa with a number of friends who'd also grown up in Sault Ste. Marie, and it turned out that of the four of us I was the only one who had known, let alone been raised by, his biological father. We partied very hard together—I had become a regular occupant of my own Drunks' Hideout—and one night we were all sitting around reminiscing about our childhoods and whose had been the harshest. We were all on acid; I had little to contribute to this conversation. Mark was recounting a boyhood where he and his brother Matt and his mother and stepfather had to scrape and scrounge cigarette money together when Rick interrupted: "Fuck that—fuck that penny-ante bullshit. That's nothing. When you spend a year of your life wandering around, not knowing where you're going... When you got no destination—no *hope*—that's when you're poor, man, that's when you're poor." So while I was playing in the CPR, collecting hockey cards and having roast beef on Sundays, Rick had been living a nightmare of loneliness and confusion and fear, possibly no more than a few blocks away. Lynn Road was not always a joyous or painless place to be a kid, but it must have been an Eden of security and continuity next to the irreparably broken homes Rick and my other friends had lived through. And so my 1972 of snow hills, St. Luke's cathedral and ten-cent bags of gumdrops was, after all, mine alone. Still, singular and subjective as my memories are, they are no less valuable to me. Lynnwood lives. When I hear people warn, Don't look back, I think to myself, Why not? I have a lovely view.

In Search Engines of Lost Time

I AM CONVINCED that one of the foremost appeals of the Internet to casual users is its function as an infinite Lost & Found, storing archives of knowledge quite useless to ninety-nine percent of the population but indispensable to the remainder—one man's junk is another man's treasure, dot com. Collectors, genealogists, and the simply curious have in electronic information an unprecedented inventory retrieval system, and there are now thousands of websites specifically designed for those seeking long-missing albums or car parts or distant relatives, or rare items needed to complete sets of antique toys or tools or musical instruments. Pornography and bootlegged pop songs attract sizable audiences too, but it is as a repository of unclaimed baggage, concrete or conceptual, that cyberspace pulls most of us in. If *The Maltese Falcon* was made today Sam Spade's detective skills would be redundant: the stuff that dreams are made of can now be tracked down by anyone with a modem and a mouse.

For many years I had my own Maltese Falcon, an issue of a comic book called *Weird War Tales* that contained the story "Fort Which Did Not Return." It had been mine when I was no more than five or six years old and my family spent summers at a cabin near Red Lake, my mother's home town in northwestern Ontario; between 1971 and 1974 "Fort Which Did Not Return" annually imprinted itself on my consciousness and thereafter, mislaid or discarded or tattered into unreadability, haunted my dreams and shaped my destiny. *Though nothing can bring back the hour / Of splendour in the grass, of glory in the flower*, could I but hold that issue of *Weird War Tales* again Red Lake and the stillness of the forest and the water and the smell of the cabin and the sleeping bags and the vision of the yellow-red twilights and my childhood would be revisited, reclaimed. As I grew older and grew up—grew further away—that comic book became a low-level obsession, an intermittent, ongoing grail; wherever I went I wondered if and how I might recover it. Over the better part of my life I looked, borne back ceaselessly into the past.

Weird War Tales was published by DC Comics (whence the more familiar *Superman, Batman, Wonder Woman*, et al.) and served as a kind of crossover bid within their catalogue, juxtaposing the guts 'n' glory settings of *Sgt. Rock* and *Our Army At War* with supernatural elements borrowed from *The House of Mystery* and *The Unexpected*. Until the final part of its run in the 80s when regular characters called The Creature Commandos and GI Robot appeared, it was an anthology series, featuring three or four self-contained narratives per issue. There was a recurring anti-war theme woven throughout them though: in a throwback to the old EC Comics line each piece was introduced by a ghoulish "host," in this case skeletal Death himself, that made for an unusually sophisticated mix of fantasy and realism. After Vietnam and assassinations, with World War II three decades gone, comics in the 70s began to shed some of their gee-whizzery, and *Weird War Tales* may have been a low-profile experiment in deepening and darkening the medium. There were no superheroes here. In *Weird War Tales* Death always won in the end.

"Fort Which Did Not Return" depicted a bombing mission of B-17 Flying Fortresses circa 1943, where one plane, nicknamed "Mother Hen" by its crew, is shot up by German fighters yet mysteriously keeps flying to reach and destroy its target. Mother Hen's sole survivor is the bombardier ("How—? *Who* took the ship over—? *How* can *Mother Hen* keep on going?") who bails out to safety, later seeing the Fort's ghost dutifully escorting his new craft on a later raid. So, it's a weird war tale. The comic itself was bequeathed to me by my older cousin Tim one Red Lake summer—he was about to enter his teens, I was about four—and soon was with me every season, at Grandma's, at the beach, at our little cottage outside of town. My father and my sister would read it to me until I could master its text myself ("TWO FIGHTERS COMING IN ON MY END—HIGH!" "BRATTAT!" "SPANG!"), gaping at the angry orange and blue panels of B-17s and Messerschmitts (I was an early appreciator of *Whaam!* and *Okay, Hot-Shot!* before I'd ever seen Roy Lichtenstein). "Fort Which Did Not Return" was pop art without the irony, World War II before World War II had become cool again. It was as much a part of my Julys and Augusts as blueberries and bug spray.

And Red Lake. Red Lake is a long way from anywhere, not least of all Mother Hen's objective of Munich, Germany: literally at the end of the Red Lake Road, a full day's drive away from either Thunder Bay to the southeast or Winnipeg to the southwest. A timber and mining town of fewer than two thousand people—large numbers of whom seemed to be related to me—its isolation in the abyss of a great coniferous ocean must have fired my imagination, must have made *Weird War Tales* a little more plausible. Or could it have been the bush planes? Red Lake's other industry is fly-in tourism, with whole squadrons of pontoon-equipped Beavers and Norsemen daily ferrying fishermen and hunters to campsites even further north; the planes themselves were of the same aeronautical vintage as Flying Fortresses and propelled by the same snarling radial engines. The fathomless Boreal horizon and the constant buzz of takeoffs and landings were my background for Mother Hen's last, fateful mission. Eventually, as our family stopped making the yearly pilgrimages and my comic book library fell into neglect, Red Lake and "Fort Which Did Not Return" combined into a single irretrievable golden age. By my ninth birthday I was a committed nostalgic.

So began my quest. Accepting that my original issue was forever gone, I undertook to find a replacement. To its exact identity I gathered clues—the child scouring his own unformed memories, the boy having just attained the age of reason grilling the pre-literate toddler he used to be. Gradually, investigating collectors' guides, I deduced that "Fort Which Did Not Return" was in fact reprinted from another magazine and included in *Weird War Tales*' debut number. A first edition! At ten, I wrote away to a comic wholesaler in the US but received no reply. Here and there, in flea markets and used book shops, I found tantalizing mid-70s copies from the series, but not the one I remembered. At twenty I left home in Sault Ste. Marie for Toronto, but the expansive Silver Snail comic emporium in that city, and its sister in my later residence of Ottawa, availed me nothing. I had the misfortune to be seeking something valuable not only to myself, and therefore likely to be prized—as first editions of anything will be—but this *Weird War Tales* was more to me than merely "collectable." There could be no price on my past. Occasional relics tormented me, like the film *Memphis Belle*, a fictionalized story of a B-17 flight inspired by William Wyler's wartime documentary, or the animated *Heavy Metal*, featuring a surreal vignette called "B-17," wherein an eponymous bomber crashes into an eerie aerial graveyard, or a Steven Spielberg-directed episode of the TV series *Amazing Stories* called "The Mission," in which cartoon undercarriage magically saves a Flying Fortress from a fatal belly landing. I felt like Ahab following Moby Dick, or Charles Foster Kane dreaming of Rosebud, or the narrator of Poe's "William Wilson," not fleeing but chasing, glimpsing in an obscure, elusive juvenile periodical "my admonisher at Eton…the destroyer of my honour at Oxford…him who thwarted my ambition at Rome, my revenge at Paris, my passionate love at Naples, or what he falsely termed my avarice in Egypt…my arch-enemy and evil genius."

Then the new century, employment at the Vancouver Public Library, and the Internet. On a lunch break or after-work whim, I'd enter "Weird War Tales" into search engines accessible at staff computer terminals, and bring up various comic book listings and indices, but little of significance. One day, though, I got a little further, into an auction site administered by Amazon.com, and found that the premiere issue I'd been stalking for almost three decades was up for sale. I had come a long way to this web page, and my dream seemed so close that I could hardly fail to grasp it. I made a couple of cautious, unsuccessful bids—higher than anyone else's, but not the seller's minimum price—and then one more, whereupon I learned that I had, indeed, agreed to buy a Very-Fine-condition *Weird War Tales* Number One, including "Fort Which Did Not Return," for seventy-five US dollars, from a Brett Rowden of San Angelo, Texas. A money order was purchased (it came to $112 Canadian, with the exchange rates of 2000), sent to the Lone Star state, and within the month I received notice that a package had arrived and was awaiting me at my local post office. On a drizzly summer afternoon I brought the thin envelope back home, opened it and the plastic wrapper within, and eased its precious cargo out from the mists of time and into the light of my adult, suburban reality. I did not know that it was already behind me, somewhere in that vast obscurity beyond the city, where the dark forests of the dominion rolled on under the night.

Of course there was a shadow of anticlimax. "Fort Which Did Not Return" was not drawn, as I'd speculated, by comic art legends Joe Kubert or Russ Heath—no credits were given at all. There were technical mistakes. Messerschmitts were described as Focke-Wulfs, and the B-17's crewmen (seven, when there should have been ten) were situated inaccurately within the airplane. Yet it was still the way I remembered, and I still saw the three-colour air battles illuminated by the cabin's candlelight, heard my father's voice reading the captions for me above the cries of loons, a spray of August rain skimming across the lake, and the day's last Norseman growling home from the wilderness at dusk: "*Lucky Lulu* is being jumped by fighters over there!" "Onward flew the battered, riddled Fort through the flaming forest of flak..." "Onward droned the ship... Out over the misty embraces of the sea... As if to a faraway land..." "Take...good care of them, *Mother Hen*..." I wondered if I'd patterned my own life, unconsciously, after the bombardier's, if I'd metaphorically parachuted away from burnt-out or screwed-up comrades, made the lone escape from the doomed bomber of my youth. And I wondered how many people are now online, pointing and clicking their way to their own *Weird War Tales*, and what will happen when they find them, when nothing they ever had and lost stays lost, when no artifact of our lives can remain idealized in tranquil restoration, and Whither is fled the visionary gleam? / Where is it now, the glory and the dream?

My search, at least, is over. Perhaps there will one day be a sort of market crash, when every stray doll, hockey card and comic book is reunited with its original owner—all those outwardly mature, even cynical, people who nevertheless harbour some secret wish to be five again, indulging themselves on the Internet until they get their gratification; perhaps only by such trivial, traceable objects are such secret wishes rewarded. I will not still search the Internet for what I can never find, not for my fifth and sixth summers, for Red Lake, for the trees and the sunsets and the silence, and not for Grandma or Dad or cousin Tim, dead of a congenital heart defect not long after he gave me his first issue of *Weird War Tales*, when we were still children. They are not being auctioned off in cyberspace. They are falling faintly through the universe and faintly falling, like the descent of their last end, but wherever they go, and whatever happens to them on the way, in that enchanted place at the top of the Forest, a little boy will always be reading "Fort Which Did Not Return," never to grow old.

Satan & Me

I HAVE ALWAYS thought the expression "It shook me to my soul" to be a particularly evocative one, conveying something beyond mere unease or disquiet and into philosophical dismay, an unsettling of spirit, moral fear. It describes the sensation I first experienced as a child, when I was unusually—I have since determined—drawn to ghost stories, the unexplained, Sasquatch and Loch Ness monster legends ("cryptozoology"), comic books like *The House of Mystery* and *Weird War Tales*, cartoon shows like *Scooby-Doo*, even, and the televangelist apocalyptics of Hal Lindsey. I was, I suppose, a sort of information age Oliver Larch, the 1889 Indiana farm boy who, in a celebrated (but possibly fictional, according to some sources) abduction case, walked outside one night to get water from his well, and was last heard calling *"They've got me!"* down to his bewildered family from the cavernous, starlit prairie sky. I was Oliver Larch myself, snatched away by the forces of the unknown forever. They'd got me too, less dramatically but just as completely, and never more completely than when, at the age of eight years, I read William Peter Blatty's *The Exorcist* cover to cover in one bright, psyche-blasting spring afternoon.

That is, of course, awfully young to have discovered such a grown-up book, one featuring murder, sexual desecration, and extensive profanity, but I came from a literate background and was never discouraged from novels or histories on the grounds of their being "too mature," or my being "a little young, yet." As a toddler I thrilled to studies of Second World War air combat, and when I turned eight I made it through Peter Benchley's *Jaws*—my first real "chapter book," I thought proudly, commencing a parent-exasperating shark kick that lasted several months (Benchley, incidentally, is an underrated writer—see his later *Lush* for some Cheeverish WASP angst). *The Exorcist*, if I recall, was something I'd simply expressed a child's curiosity for, and when an older sister came home from university she dug a copy out of her trunk, from among labyrinthine stacks of mass-market paperbacks and poli-sci texts, and obligingly bequeathed it to me. I can still hear her mock-dramatic tone as she rummaged: "The book I'm looking for is…called *The Exorcist*." She really didn't seem to think much of it; neither did I. Or was there, even then, "a chill, tugging warning," the same one Blatty's dubious Father Karras felt on first entering the house of the disturbed little girl? Was I stepping over a personal cosmic cliff when I accepted what the cover blurb called "The Bestselling Novel of Demonic Possession"? "It scraped through his bloodstream like particles of ice." Did it scrape through mine?

The Exorcist is a good, not great, piece of fiction—the only novel I can think of containing the adverb "diarrhetically"—and

William Blatty's literary reputation has never quite solidified into that of a serious author (his previous successes, in fact, had come as a writer of comic screenplays like *Promise Her Anything* and *A Shot in the Dark*). In the thirty-plus years since its debut its critical stock has found a level roughly between "publishing phenomenon" and 70s shorthand, a huge but instantly dated success, like Mario Puzo's *The Godfather* or Erich Segal's *Love Story*. Its prologue in northern Iraq and its scenes of kindly Catholic priests entrusted with the aid of a young child are seen in a much different light eventful decades later. Detractors remember it as blood and thunder for the Me Decade, analysts see a symbol-laden parable of intergenerational conflict, defenders are scarce—is there anything as embarrassing to admit as a long-ago suspension of disbelief? Other than a digitally souped-up re-release of the film in 2000, *The Exorcist* was last in the public spotlight during the Clarence Thomas-Anita Hill hearings, in 1991, when suspicions were raised that Hill had cribbed some of her sexual harassment allegations from Blatty's novel—specifically a charge that echoed the character Burke Dennings' drunken observation, "There seems to be an alien pubic hair floating round in my gin." Clarence Thomas, you suave devil. There is a surreal photograph from the hearings of Senator Orrin Hatch solemnly brandishing a hardcover edition of *The Exorcist* like a holy book. To me it is.

Respectable literature, pop culture landmark, or perjury-proving potboiler, *The Exorcist* permanently unnerved me at my initial encounter, and to this day I still pick up my copy—the same one I held white-knuckled in 1976, now frayed and dog-eared past all redemption—and flip through its deepest, darkest passages: Captain Howdy, the invisible playmate suddenly turned hostile, chasing Regan MacNeil downstairs as she cowers away and shrieks "There he is!" at the vacant kitchen doorway; her bed rising up during the exorcism, "bobbing and listing gently as if it were floating on a stagnant lake"; Father Merrin explaining, "the point is to make us despair; to reject our own humanity...to see ourselves as ultimately bestial; as ultimately vile and putrescent"; the eerie voice spilling inverted from within and without Regan, calling from the void "*Nowonmai... nowonmai*" —"I am no one." Whatever else it may be, that is effective scare-mongering. I was about as old as Regan herself when I read it, remember, and it struck me not so much as a horror story but as a cautionary docudrama, a plausible narrative of supernatural reality, something that *could happen to me*. I'd never shoot down a Heinkel in the Battle of Britain, I knew, and I'd probably never harpoon a Great White Shark, but there was nothing to prevent Captain Howdy creeping out of the abyss to hunt me down in my bed. I wanted to fast-forward to the strength and skepticism of adulthood, which children often wish and which never happens to them. *They've got me!*

And this was in the 70s, too, the aftermath of Altamont and Manson and Watergate, and Ira Levin's *Rosemary's Baby* and *The Exorcist*, book and movie, itself—the devil's business appeared very visible then, and it wasn't difficult to explore the subject of disembodied malevolent intelligences interfering in human affairs. I went from Blatty's fiction to William Friedkin's film, bowdlerized for TV—"Your mother still rots [sucks cocks] in hell"—but still terrifying, alone in the house when I saw it, and thence to Jay Anson's *The Amityville Horror* (probably another fraud, I have since learned), reams of witchcraft and poltergeist lore, stolen glimpses at Anton LaVey's *The Satanic Bible* in the local book store, and parapsychologist D. Scott Rogo's *The Haunted Universe*, which quoted the following recollection from psychiatrist Dr. Arthur Guirdham:

> I do not know exactly my age when I had my first Satanic experience. As near as I can say I was six or seven. I was lying in my bed when I felt drawn and horrified by a presence outside my bedroom. I rose from my bed, magnetised by the unseen horror, and opened the door of my room. What I saw was unforgettable. I first noticed his face... It was covered with a close-woven blue-grey pelt... His smile was not only diabolic but welcoming... He did not have human feet... I was so hypnotized by his face and his evil smile that I did not look closely at his feet. I know now that he had hooves...

I was ten years old! Even now, settled, adult, responsible, a flash of some distant inner fright nags at me when I open a door in my home. Why shouldn't some hateful alien being choose this moment to manifest itself to me, a surprise Satanic experience waiting on the other side, and say "You were right, I've been here all along, and now here I am"? Who? "Nowonmai."

Back then this all fell under the category of "The Occult," which always had a nostalgic, Old World element of tradition and superstition about it; nowadays such material has been largely pushed aside by "New Age" banalities, with angels and ETs replacing demons and disappearances as paranormal titillation for the masses. Our loss, I think. Satan no longer has a genre to himself. But *The Exorcist* caught me at the right time, and I will always be more loyal to it than the watered-down mysticism of *The Celestine Prophecy*, the junk conspiracy theories of *The X-Files*, and the crap "media savvy" of *The Blair Witch Project* and *Scream*. The novel plunged like a stone into my preadolescent aesthetic, radiating outward over time to encompass Edgar Allan Poe, H.P. Lovecraft, Stephen King (at his best a fine writer, but very rarely at his best), Aleister Crowley, M.C. Escher, Teilhard de Chardin (the visionary Jesuit paleontologist, and model for Father Merrin), Goya, Henry Fuseli, marijuana, LSD, Shirley Jackson, Algernon Blackwood, Gustave Doré, Kiss (Knights *In* Satan's Service, longstanding rumor has it), AC/DC (Anti-Christ, *D*own with Christ—less plausible, to my mind), Black Sabbath (there's a glorious picture of Sabbath backstage circa 1975, singer Ozzy Osbourne cradling a nubile *Exorcist* star Linda Blair, like a blasphemous Tarzan and Jane), and, not least of all, Jesus Christ himself. For the ultimate message of *The Exorcist* must be that, while evil surely exists, skulking through eternity in what Lovecraft called "the mad spaces between the stars," so too does good, whether the Christian or some other acknowledged kind; as William Peter Blatty put it, after reading the 1949 *Washington Post* article that inspired his work, "If there were demons, there were angels and probably a God and a life everlasting." At the story's climax Father Merrin suggests, "Perhaps evil is the crucible of goodness... And perhaps even Satan—Satan in spite of himself—somehow serves to work out the will of God." Perhaps he did for me.

I hesitate to say *The Exorcist* was some kind of Gen X touchstone, because the people I knew who shared my appreciation of it were more like a small sect of believers, acolytes, invoking it at special times and generally going further out than most readers or moviegoers on the tangent we thought of as the Satan trip. "Praise be to Pazuzu," we'd say, thanking Regan MacNeil's possessor at any instance of good fortune; or, speculating how best to offend a born-again co-worker, we'd cite Regan with her crucifix: "*Let Jesus fuck you!*" In those days pop culture had not yet become its own chief subject, as it has now, and so the novel and movie seemed to cut through all the product of the entertainment-industrial complex to speak of a deeper, truer existence than the one pushed by the trendspotters, more serious and more lasting. They weren't just fads or hits, but the mechanics of the universe revealed. Re-reading the book or re-watching the film came to feel like a solemn annual observance, somehow autumnal, like going back to school or raking dead leaves or feeling the encroaching cold and dark, or like Halloween. Alternately, a brisk, sunlit day in March or April would take me back to the time of my first *Exorcist* experience—a promise of rebirth qualified by wind and melting snow and barren trees against the desolate blue sky. My friend Todd would cue up his video to the scene where Pazuzu has Regan levitating high above her bed while the exorcists shout her downward, beseeching "The power of Christ compels you!" "Twenty years later, man," Todd would say admiringly, "and it still doesn't get any heavier." Right on. Another guy, a heavy metal buff and occasional cannabis merchant, once showed me his own well-worn *Exorcist*: "You've read this, haven't you?" "Oh, shit, yeah," I answered. "The father of us all."

Imagine me at nine years old, then, still reeling from my introduction to the book a few months before, cringing under the covers in the black of night, gone without a decent sleep for weeks, feeling vulnerable like never before or since to the ghastly, nameless entities that hid—and still hide—among the everyday atoms of this surface, material world. Nine, I was, literally praying for safety from Pazuzu and Captain Howdy and whatever hovered silently in the walls and above and around my bed. Most nights I would eventually drift off, but once I remember distinctly, in the extremity of my fear, feeling a single *tug at my foot*, fleeting but firm, as if all the panic that had been welling up in my boyish awareness took solid form and made a grab for me. That must have been it, obviously, a moment of autosuggestion or hypersensitivity, or the family cat; it couldn't have been anything else, sniffing a child's terror like blood and trying to make off with him like Oliver Larch, yanking him into the endless nightmare wasteland where Nowonmai dwelt. No, that couldn't have been it, but that one desperate clutch still lingers as a physical memory, the peak of the hope and dread that was brought to me, and which I still carry about in my mundane, waking life, by *The Exorcist*. That shook me to my soul. That shook me to my soul.

Pikangikum

IN ONE OF my last summers at Red Lake I was old enough to go out on my own during the daytime, and so I would often walk down the road from Grandma's place where we were staying to the floatplane docks at Green Airways. This was one of the town's oldest fly-in fishing operators, comprising six or seven single- and twin-engined aircraft, all painted yellow with green trim on the wingtips, and as the owners were old acquaintances of our family they didn't mind me hanging around; they had even given us short aerial circuits around the lake in years past. Now I was just happy to watch the planes come and go, carrying campers and equipment out from Red Lake to one of Green's little resorts in the surrounding district, isolated cabins accessible only by air. Once, however, I must have been looking more longingly than usual at the arrivals and departures and I got noticed. A Cessna was being loaded up and I heard someone say, "Take the little boy for a ride."

Before I had time to hesitate I was climbing aboard the bush plane, a four-seater, and I was told not to worry, that my parents would be notified of where I was and that I would be back before long. It was to be just a quick trip. Inside were two old Indians and a youngish pilot in a baseball cap. This was evidently just a routine charter flight, travelling not to a fishing lodge but to the Indian reserve of Pikangikum a hundred miles north; the native people seemed to be bringing some boxes or bags of goods they'd bought in Red Lake and were returning home, I guess. One of them, I remember, was carrying a child's tricycle as the biggest item. The Cessna started up with a whine and a sputter—the motor and the propeller were just outside the front windscreen—and we began to taxi out onto the lake. In a minute the pilot turned into the wind and pushed the throttle in; the rear of the plane tilted down and the spray of water, more than any displaced by the fastest speedboat, was splashing over the pontoons and up to the side windows. And then we were flying. I was by myself. I was nine years old.

For the sheer frequency of flights in and out, Red Lake's centre of Howey Bay has been considered the busiest airport in the world: think of O'Hare in Chicago or Heathrow in London shrunk down to a freshwater lake on the Canadian Shield, with transcontinental Airbuses and Boeings recast as waterborne Beechcraft and de Havillands. Think too of the terrain being flown over: lakes and ponds and muskeg and rivers, far as the eye can see, so that it is impossible to distinguish whether it is the mainland interrupted by water, or if you are looking down on an infinite archipelago of small pine-covered islands in a clear shallow sea. Bush pilots and their machines are often credited with "opening up" Canada's north in the early twentieth century, but even decades later there was still a lot of landscape where no white man had ever set down—just scattered stations named Sioux Lookout, Ear Falls, Lac Seul or Wabigoon, and ragged, rocky pools called Pakwash Lake, Bloodvein River, Vermilion Bay, or Nungesser Lake and Coli Lake, the latter two named in honor of two French aviators whose plane had been lost over the Atlantic in 1927. This was the region now passing a few thousand feet under me on a late summer afternoon in 1976. I was shy and uncertain and had my fingers crossed, against what I wasn't sure. The Indians, a wrinkled and silent pair of grandparents, saw my nervousness and smiled kindly, and I smiled back.

Within an hour we touched down at Pikangikum. This was not a small town like Red Lake, visible from the air as an obviously populated community of buildings, vehicles, and roadways, but a meagre field on a sandy beach, and a solitary dock stuck out into the water. I saw only some small prefabricated housing blocks grouped in the distance; I couldn't detect anything like streets or stores. It was a grey afternoon and as the Cessna putted up to the dock a gaggle of locals waited for us. The two elderly passengers deplaned and the pilot helped them with their possessions. There was some kind of language barrier between him and the others, all of them natives, who had come to greet the seniors—"This plane can only hold four people," the pilot was repeating to them. "This plane can only hold four people." Somehow a few new passengers came on board and we taxied across the lake at just under takeoff speed to another worn pier a couple of minutes away, until these people, apparently satisfied with a quick lift around the reserve, got off themselves, leaving me and the pilot alone. We left the settlement behind and roared up off the water.

The flier, who seemed to be no more than twenty-five, introduced himself as we flew back to Red Lake. "I'm Peter," he told me. "Peter the pilot," I said, and he nodded with appreciation. "I hope we got enough gas," I told him, less out of real concern than as a way to show interest, although of course I was excited the whole trip. "Aw, we've got plenty of gas," he replied, nonchalant—this was, presumably, just another puddle-jump for him, another couple of hours in his logbook. Looking out the windows I had no idea where we were or what our bearings were: it was only when we were descending, as I recognized a little service station on the highway leading into Red Lake, that I realized how remote both base and destination had been, and how small the little Cessna was against the taigan panorama of trees and lakes and clouds. We landed right into Howey Bay—bush planes are prized for their ability to get in and out of small airstrips, whether on floats, skis, or wheels—and returned to the Green Airways wharf, as Peter cut the engine and the aircraft drifted in, its propeller safely motionless while he and some dockhands guided us to a halt and secured lines to the pontoons. My parents were waiting for me (my mother had taken the call from Green's just in time to see me taking off outside Grandma's windows) and they thanked the pilot and the owner for indulging a kid's unspoken wish and, perhaps, for taking me off their hands for a few hours. I was always bugging them about model airplanes, toy airplanes, airplane comics, airplane drawings, and airplane movies.

Some of my strongest memories of spending vacations at Red Lake are of being seated in a car as we drove in and out of town: from a child's point of view, the perspective is not out and over the hood but up and towards the silhouette of pine trees that lined the side of the road for hour after hour. I can also recall my mother and father's 8-track tapes we'd play while driving, swing music by Artie Shaw or Glenn Miller or Tommy Dorsey, so that the clarinet of "Begin the Beguine" or the brass of "In the Mood" always takes me back to the hush of summer evenings in northwestern Ontario, as if the bush and the rocks were so eternal they were actually tugging us back in history, at least to the Big Band era. The Red Lake region is designated "Sunset Country" in tour guides, and the sunsets there are indeed lingering and maybe a little lonely, for when night comes to that part of the world you will see how few and faint the lights of civilization are on the darkness of earth. But I also think back to one summer vacation and remember that flight in the yellow and green Cessna, and the citizens of the Pikangikum Indian Reserve, who were not on holiday and who did not get treated to joyrides in a bush plane. As far as they knew they had lived there forever; they had no eternity to revisit because they still resided in one, or were trying to. A nine-year-old white boy had once come from the south to them for a few minutes and would recollect it far into the future, but those who stayed in Pikangikum soon resumed their impassive, aboriginal existence at the shore of time.

The Most Perfect Moment

YEARS LATER, AT twenty or twenty-five, he would still be able to recall it—a trivial, childish childhood memory that but for some stubborn little synapse or neuron would have been forgotten a week after it happened—and he would still feel that flicker of satisfaction. Never enough to seriously lift his mood or even bring forth the faintest smile, but though it did not really mean much (didn't mean anything, really), it was still supremely good and true, a tribute to everything he thought was strong and able within himself.

How many others like this one had there been? A few seconds here, a few seconds there, certainly a thousand happy recollections of friends or lovers or any kind of absurd little experience, and some of them not absurd at all, that were just as pleasant to think back on and often more meaningful in the course of his life. But this one remained, not for being better than any of the others (what was better than catching the jackfish off the end of the dock in Red Lake while his father scrambled for the net? The first seconds of his own Super-8 film projected on the living room wall? Selling that first short story? Being stoned and jamming with Dan as the chords and licks came together under the sun? Waking up beside Gail after a fine fall night together?) but for being complete unto itself. There were times when he thought this was the last wholly positive thing he'd ever known, the last time in almost two decades that it had all worked out for the best.

*

He'd been about ten or eleven years old when it happened, in Grade Six at Alex Muir Public School in the Sault. Deep, cold winter; a January afternoon that was already full of long shadows by the 2:45 recess. The playground, that great expansive landscape to anyone under five feet tall, was full of little people: a handful huddled close by the doors and talking with the teachers, a couple of dozen way out in the field by the snowed-over basketball courts, Grade Ones and Twos on the monkey bars, a few on the rink, some on the snow hills, a small city of small human beings going about its daily business. Kids.

He and his friends were playing tag. Tag! The greatest game ever invented. No—the greatest game ever evolved from centuries of primal chasing and stalking and killing, the deadly instincts of hunter and prey handed down from cavemen to barbarians to soldiers to schoolchildren. No equipment but speed and cunning, no violence but a gentle swat of a hand across another's back. For six or seven young boys, the schoolyard was an epic battleground on that day: they ran and outran each other, invested with the courage and camaraderie of crusading knights or samurai warriors. No one ever said, "Let's play a game of tag," for it was no game. There was only that opening ritual of legs and feet stretched out into a tiny circle, a random counting-off to some ancient rhythmic singsong...

"*Bubblegum, bubblegum, in a dish, how many bubblegum do you wish?*" The gloved finger pointed at Darren's boot.

"Six."

"One-two-three-four-five-six." Around the finger went.

And then Scott was It, the first hunter who would catch another and build up an ever-expanding team of allies until the last victim was outpaced and trapped and snared. The circle broke up and trotted off in pairs or singles or triples, each one ready to sprint, each one keeping watch.

In ten minutes the group was spread out over the yard. And he had already been caught, bested by a briefly more agile classmate, ambushed by swiftness. But there were no causes here, no victors or vanquished. There were only targets and those who found targets, Caught and Uncaught. They were constantly cruising at a light gallop (under heavy parkas, yet—impossible for him five or ten years hence), and, searching out more objectives, he and two teammates met by a far fence and came up with a strategy.

"Who's left?"

"Kevin, Butler, and S."

"'Kay, I'll take Butler."

"I think Kevin's near the backstop—yeah..."

"I'm on S," he said. "There he is now." The three hounds jogged off towards their foxes.

Craig Smythe, "Craig S" to the teachers, merely "S" to his friends, could be seen ambling briskly across the field toward the snow hill, hoping no doubt to lose himself in the knots of pupils standing or sliding around there, a classic manoeuvre—the elemental quarry disappearing into the forest. S had seen his tracker see *him*, and he knew he was in gunsights. S picked up speed, a whirl of legs and elbows, buck teeth and freckles.

The hunter was moving fast, too, but the distance was too great and the warning was too early. He was locked into pursuit mode, though, and surely S knew that; there was no chance for him yet, but he would make it come.

He watched S scamper up and over the tip of the snow hill nearest a private backyard, and now his mind clicked into calculations and projections and that ingrained killing impulse he would never as freely use again. If he cut around the hill's near side into the area closest to the school's entrance he would undoubtedly head S off—but coming at him from in front rather than behind, in plain view. It would give S an opportunity to simply dart out of his reach and leave him out of position. The option was considered and ruled out in a second.

So, while still a fair range behind, and now not even seeing him, he decided to follow S's route around the hill, to stay on his tail. He was running at a good clip now, a small boy in mittens and a hat that his mother had knit for him, running with a purpose he would never again know in his life.

He emerged on the other side of the snow hill to a crowd of older kids idling about, blocking all forward vision. Where was S? More calculations, more targeting. If he went among and through the gaggles of bystanders he would be slowed down, stumbling over ice-boulders and other obstacles; that may have been S's trail but he guessed himself close enough behind him to swing out to the open area by the teachers' parking lot and lock in on his kill. He was there in a few loping steps, and he searched for S's back.

He found it.

There was S, moving easier now, thinking that he had eluded the hound. His internal computer had accurately predicted S's behaviour: he had run between the older kids and the hill, and assumed his pursuer was still somewhere in the open field. S's head swung forward and left, forward and left, looking for the one he thought he had escaped, not knowing that doom was coming up behind and to the right of him.

Doom. Because now S was not S, who sat a couple of rows away from him and who he traded hockey cards with—now S was de Havilland DH9A light bomber, and he was Enemy Ace zooming down from the clouds on his unsuspecting victim, a World War I dogfight scenario taken from a favourite comic book; it applied perfectly now. Out of the clouds in his beautiful Fokker triplane, finger on the gun-button, no longer a child playing tag with a school friend, no longer a boy with messy orange hair who always felt a twinge of fear at the beginning of a math lesson and its cryptic menace of fractions and long division—no longer. The most perfect moment loomed before him like an open doorway.

Enemy Ace, in comic balloons splayed across the page: "*I will not need tracers…*"

"*…to guide me…*"

"*…at this close range…*"

He gained on S with a vicious joy, undetected and unhurried. Running, yes, but not really chasing. He was but a few paces away this second, and S grew larger in his sights, still glancing over nervously to where no one was. At the end he did turn and see his fatal mistake, but to no avail. S put on a burst of speed, but he was a target.

Enemy Ace stretched out his arm, the mittened fingers slapped the parka-ed back, and the DH9A light bomber burst into flames.

*

He would never remember the rest of that recess, and indeed with time most of those years were misted over, all the other recesses and how ever many hundred triumphs and defeats, all the other times he had put out his hand and brushed someone's back while playing tag. It was just that once.

That once. It remained as a fleeting thought, as fast as he had run that day, as bright as the sinking sun on that frigid afternoon of his eleventh year. Since those last few steps when S had looked left and then forward and then understood and looked back— nothing had been quite as full or as complete. It had not changed anything or led anywhere, of course, but as he had grown up and older, and soon enough would grow old, the beautiful memory lingered and it would always pass through his mind like a dear friend, cheering him a little when it stopped by and leaving a minute gift of gladness in his heart.

Part II

Fire-Swept, Algoma

Mine

PRONTO WAS A trip. Fall 1985. Just out of high school and time on our hands. Hanging out with Chris Bradshaw and Dan Duggan: Chris was employed as basically a live-in babysitter for two young boys, and when their father went to work the night shift at the steel plant Chris would see that the kids got to bed okay, and then settle down to play his classical guitar and paint and read and call Dan and me over to smoke hash oil. "Take hold of the soul hole," was his usual invitation, and he shared with his friends what he always called his "personal." There Chris and Dan and I would recite *The Rime of the Ancient Mariner* to each other, check out Chris's canvases of surreal architecture, laugh at *The Terminator* and *Repo Man* on pay-TV, warm up with shots of chilled aquavit, and smoke oil until it got to be three or four bells.

Chris introduced us to Scott Muller who mentioned an abandoned mine he knew about just east of Blind River, and we agreed to make a day of exploring the place. "A demo party," Chris hoped, and a decent road trip, if nothing else. It was to be both boyhood adventure and adult risk, outdoor fun and testosterone-driven vandalism, exactly the sort of thing you'd do if you were an eighteen-year-old male in Sault Ste. Marie with access to a vehicle and plenty of drugs. Hunter S. Thompson does the District of Algoma.

We met early one autumn Saturday: me, Chris, Dan, Muller (but we called him "Merv," after a pair of Indians Chris had met named Merv and Dona), and Jason White, who we called White Lightning. Chris was driving the Bradshaw family car, a big Chrysler, and we took our seats and started driving east down Trunk Road. It was a cool, grey morning as we made a quick stop at Churchill Plaza, where Mike Horchuk was waiting in his truck. He had the hash oil and the acid. A quick transaction was made in the empty parking lot, and then we headed out of the city, into the rising October sun.

Chris, Dan, and Merv took acid, and White Lightning assumed the joint-rolling responsibilities. My job, beside Chris in the driver's seat, was to be a kind of chemical co-pilot, keeping watch on the speedometer and any road hazards that the hallucinating Chris might not notice—as the hits kicked in I had to confirm to our chauffeur that he was neither going at a thousand miles per hour nor standing still, depending on the point in his inner trip. Meanwhile the joints started going around as Merv told us what Pronto was, exactly.

His family had a camp nearby, he explained, and he'd discovered the site some time before. It was in fact a branch unit of the larger Pronto uranium mines, which were based in Elliot Lake, and had evidently been deserted for lack of worthwhile minerals. It was now pretty much gutted of useful equipment and most of the entrances had been sealed off by chain-link fence. "To keep the bears out," was his hypothesis. So we would not be trespassing, quite, just checking out a derelict, if still technically private, place that was now left to the elements. Meanwhile, Chris was trying to relight a spliff with the car's automatic lighter. "How's it coming?" I asked him. "Not too cool," he said, and we all laughed. "Not too cool," I started repeating, but he advised me, "Don't kill it."

The drive took over an hour, through Garden River, Echo Bay, Desbarats, Bruce Mines, and Iron Bridge, curving through the seasonal foliage and catching glimpses of Lake Huron's North Channel between the trees and hills. We got through the small town of Blind River and saw a dead cat on the side of the highway. "I like cats," I said in sympathy, and Dan asked why I then didn't get out and fuck it. Hilarity ensued. Merv pointed out the turnoff to Pronto, a nondescript dirt road, and soon we were heading north over gravel and potholes, taking an enormous bump at one point that completely fried Chris out. In a few minutes the bush on either side of us opened up, and we were at the mine.

I had imagined nothing more than a windblown shack over a dark, deep cave, like something out of *The Treasure of the Sierra Madre*, but we were actually driving up to a small industrial complex: there were several factory-sized buildings situated around a central "street," and one of the structures held a tall tower that might once have been the headframe. A little lake was at the far side of the development, and a rocky cliff stood at its southern edge. Pronto, or whatever its official title was, resembled a ghost town, somewhere that could clearly have in the past been filled with trucks and workers and activity but which was now a desolate footprint the nuclear age had left passing through northern Ontario. It was what Merv said it was, an abandoned uranium mine. It was a bit eerie.

We strolled around a while to get the lay of the land. Someone noticed a long pipe extending from one of the structures and ending in the water nearby, next to a sign saying "DANGER—HAZARDOUS WASTE." Black comedy. Some of the lake already showed signs of chemical discoloration, and I suggested it was part of God's palette, drawing more lysergic laughs. We ascended the Cambrian heights on the fringe of the area, where we relaxed to get a view of the highway and the water in the distance. The acid was now at full potency, and I launched into speculations about the extraterrestrial origin of the geology where we reclined, like Rod Serling in one of those *In Search Of* documentaries: "Because the rocks have no sign of human manufacture, they must have come from outer space..." I stopped when I saw Chris, Dan and Merv were giggling uncontrollably at this, and for months afterward all I had to say was *"Because the rocks..."* to set them off again. It was only topped by a later LSD observation of Merv's, "I wonder what a seagull's thinking right now." Then we went back down to investigate Pronto proper.

Chris and Dan did karate in Sault Ste. Marie and, now full of adrenalin and other compounds, were eager to practice their kicks on the plaster drywall of the mine. They started blasting holes everywhere while Merv and White Lightning and I ventured further inside, smashing windows occasionally to remain in the spirit. The first building we were in was a large open plant, two or three storeys high and laced with steel catwalks, piping, and girders; the Battle of Stalingrad could've been re-enacted there. The only light came from the few empty windows and holes in the roof. At one point I was walking uncertainly down a metal bridge when I stepped in a rain puddle that reflected the sky above, and for a sickening second I thought I had walked into a gap in the steel and was about to fall twenty or thirty feet, but it was just a trick of the dark. When Chris and Dan had demolished as much plaster as they could find we emerged on the other side of the facility, slightly disoriented from the maze of stairs and corridors we had just been through. "Where did we come from?" Chris asked, and Dan put in, "Who are we? Why are we here?"

Next we crossed the mine's main roadway to the other edifices. I seem to remember climbing a very tall and rickety step ladder up the headframe, where an enormous crow had built a nest. The bird circled and cawed furiously—I could see it and the sky way above me, through spaces in the roof and walls—and I crept back down. We now seemed to be in the administrative area of Pronto, winding our way through offices and lockers and storage units as Chris and Dan kept kicking things. Someone remarked that it all looked like a backdrop for some post-apocalyptic rock video, and there were vague plans to return with my Super-8 movie camera. Indeed, in some places it resembled a great stage set for a science fiction movie, the shattered remains of headquarters or a fortress or civilization itself. In others there was a *Mary Celeste* apprehension around every corner, as if the foremen and engineers had just stepped out, leaving their blueprints and papers on worktables and desks, to return any moment and find five young burnouts trashing their way through it. We had just about made a complete circuit of the buildings when we emerged onto a flat roof that looked down upon Pronto's street, sitting to rest and smoke another doob. Chris related an anecdote about himself and some other guys once selling someone a "joint" filled with gunpowder, but then his story trailed off. "Well, what happened?" we asked. "I dunno," Chris replied, as if that was the prank's least interesting part. "I guess it went off in his face." He stopped to reflect on this and we all laughed again.

It was time to go. The acid trip was subsiding, and we got back in the Chrysler for the journey back to the Sault; it was after 3:00 in the afternoon and we'd been partying several hours. We came back out to the highway and noticed a dude on the shoulder of the road with his thumb out. "Hey," we all yelled, in a fit of stoned inspiration, "let's pitch up a hick-hiker!" Chris swerved over to the side, but the hitchhiker saw who we were and what we were likely on, and he quickly withdrew his hand and turned away. No passengers for the trek back. We crossed a bridge over a slow meandering course of water, and I said I guess that's why it's called Blind River. On the other side of Blind River, the town, we had to get some gas. "Hey, I'm tryin' to roll a spliff here," complained White Lightning as the car rocked into the Mom 'n' Pop station, and the kid who filled the tank looked in at us, puzzled and uneasy. We stepped out, dishevelled and covered in dust, and went into the little eatery or convenience store or whatever it was. We were still quite high, and suddenly it was like *Easy Rider*, the longhaired city freaks walking into the country diner. "*Well, you walk into a restaurant, strung out from the road / And you feel the eyes upon you as you're shaking off the cold...*" as in the Bob Seger song. Dan tried to play a game of pinball while the rest of us bought some snacks. He was wired and started to shake the thing violently while the regular customers looked on, saying nothing. "What you represent to them is freedom," says Jack Nicholson in the biker classic. Whatever.

In Sault Ste. Marie again by late afternoon we parked the car and drifted around, decompressing. At that age we had energy and inquisitiveness enough that there was still room for further exploits wherever the remainder of the day might take us, so Chris and Merv and I wound up in the recreation room of a high-rise apartment building, where somebody knew a girl from high school. We considered a dart board there, and I noted how I'd posted Ronald Reagan's image on the one at my home. "I've got Michael Jackson on mine," said Merv, and we shared a chuckle. Now our bond ran deep.

I only went to Pronto once more, although I think Chris and Merv were there on several occasions—Chris in particular liked the nuclear wasteland aspect of the scene, the chemical spillage, the rusting hulks of mechanization, and the Ontario wilderness slowly encroaching back into the steel and bricks and concrete. For a long while after I wondered if there was any danger in our spending so much time among all that potentially toxic material—this was a uranium mine, and who knew how much of what we broke into and clambered over was radioactive?—but at last report none of us have died premature deaths, and some of us have kids, so it must have been all right.

The Four Freaks

―――――

Dr. Moreau...was the primary officiant at the monthly meetings. From a crystal vase he would dispense a spoonful of green hashish paste, pronouncing the dictum, "This will be deducted from your share in paradise." These meetings were held regularly and conducted with the formality of a religious service.
—William Emboden, *Narcotic Plants*

There was a time everything was fine
You got drunk on the day like it was wine
And all the children, they put flowers in their hair
And all the grownups, they put daggers in their stares...
—T-Rex, "Raw Ramp"©

NONE OF THIS is unique, or important, but it is all true.

*

IT IS VERY LATE, and outside it is very cold. Winter has come down hard, not with a soft and friendly dump of snow but with a stinging, glacial chill and a dry wind that makes your ears hurt. There hasn't been much snow at all this year; the pavement of the little street is exposed and raw, and the pale orange glow of the streetlight accentuates the icy bleakness of the scene. The sky is mostly clear, with a full moon high and distant. Most of the houses—fairly old, mid-sized family dwellings—are dark and restful. But one of these buildings is a seemingly unfinished place, the ugly yellow of its exterior siding contrasting sharply with the homey appearance of its neighbours, and from an upper window a tired glimmer of light is still visible through curtains, stubbornly refusing to die.

The apartment is small but not too small, neither spacious nor stuffy. "Cozy" is perhaps the most suitable adjective here, even though the decor is not quite that of an English tea-room: posters and mirrors and burlap wall hangings are prominent, celebrating the Beatles, the Rolling Stones, Pink Floyd, and other rock groups. Images of dragons and demons are scattered about, as are paperback books, magazines, and houseplants. A Confederate flag—a rebel flag—is on the bathroom door. The lighting is dim and the whole place is smoky, but the atmosphere is not foreboding—rather, the earth tones of the carpeting and the worn wooden furnishings combine with the low illumination to give this central area (the hall and the living room, which are first seen upon mounting the stairs and turning towards the front of the house) an overall tint of faded, fading amber.

Four young men are here. They are wearily rising from their positions around a cluttered coffee table, two of them lurching up off a comfortable-looking couch, one straining out of a deep, luxurious easy chair, the fourth lifting himself—wearily, wearily—from his angular seat near a corner by the window and removing a big black cat from his lap. Except for their occasional hushed curses and grunts and coughs they are quiet; outside the odd car or two can be heard far away, and deeply whistling gusts of wind. A feeling of aftermath hangs over everything. The four slowly move towards the stairs which lead down to the door.

While they are all of roughly equal height—not imposingly tall or big, though they dominate the narrow corridor enough to make it seem almost crowded—they are nonetheless distinct in their features and their manners. The lank, hollow-cheeked, curly-maned fellow is slouched near a bookcase, his arms folded and his bright azure eyes bloodshot (the clash of blue and red is almost pretty) and sunk deep into his skull. Close to him, slightly shorter, a bespectacled, bewhiskered redhead shakily dons a parka, scarf, and gloves. His hair is long and thick and without a discernible style—it is only a mass of dull orange. Behind this one, buttoning his coat, slipping on his gloves and tying his scarf, is a boyish, smiling guy who wears round John Lennon glasses. His sandy, stringy strands hang straight and he seems the most alert of the group. Bringing up the rear, already wearing his black overcoat, stands a hard-faced and sturdy figure, legs apart, with blonde hair that is shorter than the others'. He strokes the cat as it pads along the low wall of the stairwell. These three who are dressed for the cold file past the one who is staying and exchange brief, mumbled goodbyes before they walk heavily down the steps and out the door.

"Pretty good scene tonight, man... One for the record books."

"Yep... Fer-fuckin'-sure."

"Take it easy, Doug—I'll be by tomorrow."

"Good enough, man, take it easy."

"I'll bring that book."

"Whatever, man."

"See ya around... Thanks for the smokage."

"See you later, man... Don't let the cat get out."

Outside now, in the frigid February night, they have passed through a little porch, out the front door, down a couple of stairs and out into the empty street. Some chatting. More goodbyes.

"Shit, am I ever fuckin' stoned."

"Oh, fuck..."

"Dan, you can't come to my place."

"No? Well buddy, what time are you getting up?"

"Most likely when you come and wake me up, as you undoubtedly will."

"Well, I gotta head, lads... Catch you on the flip side."

"Why don't you come my way, man?"

"Naw, I gotta fuckin' move, man... Hey, that's a good tune, eh?"

"Oh, yeah, that's a fuckin' great tune—I can just see him fuckin' wailing..."

"Yeah, classic 70s hard rock, eh? Well, take 'er easy, Matt, you freak."

"Ehh."

"Oh, come on, man, I'll just drop by for a bit."

"No, fuck off, I wanna get some sleep."

"Okay, well, I'll be by tomorrow."

"I'm sure you will."

"See you later, Tom."

"Yeah, see you guys later... Fuckin' good scene."

"Right on."

They are alone now.

*

IT WAS DURING the previous summer that the four of them had come together in Sault Ste. Marie. Collectively they called themselves the four freaks; individually they were Doug, Tom, Dan and Matt.

Doug Davis was a gaunt and grim twenty-one, a struggling author who had once written, "I've seen a bit of everything, some things I haven't seen enough of, some things I never want to see again." Doug read a lot, and he played the flute, and he enjoyed chess, and he dreamed of living in Greece, and he was heavily into the spiritual. He went through many hand-rolled cigarettes of Drum tobacco and he wore a skull ring. He hated all authority.

Mopheaded Tom Howe, nineteen, was unkempt and brainy in the classic manner of the absent-minded professor. Cautious and conservative, sensitive yet sardonic (his wit was not so much dry as parched), he too was an avid reader, as well as an artist, writer, guitar player, and aspiring filmmaker. Tom was always apologizing, and spoke very articulately. He prayed nightly, and he chewed his nails to the quick.

Sixteen-year-old Dan Tremblay was a cheerful sort who was pleasant to everyone and good-humoured about most things except for the United States, Ronald Reagan, and his mother's boyfriend, who he mostly referred to as "Slime." Like Tom he played guitar (he could play flute and recorder also) and had a strong sentimental streak. One of his big heroes was Abbie Hoffman, the revolutionary youth leader of the 60s—his interest in that decade had him using catchphrases like "Hey, man," "Peace and love," and "God is acid." Dan always offered his friends tea when they were at his place.

Matt Wright, who was seventeen, was a pessimist and a cynic. He had a rat-a-tat-tat way of talking and an aggressive, ironic, caustic sense of humor. A master of dialects and expressions, he could spontaneously act out any of a range of "characters" that included demons, soldiers, evangelists, and drunken Indians. The deadpan, unsettling performances sometimes seemed close to split personality. A solid, tanklike guy who looked kind of like the movie actor Willem Dafoe, Matt was usually hungry, and he smoked a lot.

*

DOUG DAVIS and Tom Howe by that time had been constant companions for nearly six years. They had met at Alex Muir public school, and continued on to Sir James Dunn high school together—but unlike the principals of many such friendships, Doug and Tom had remained as close outside the school walls as in. (In a short first-person account of the time, Doug wrote "We have a lot of fun walking home from school. It almost makes it worth going to school in the first place.") They had raised various forms of hell while getting their educations. Doug would get suspended for weeks on end, make sinister prank calls to the principal ("*Hey Frank... Got your dog, Frank... Yeah... Fucked it good, too...*"), and he and Tom and some other guys annually hung effigies of school administrators off the building's roof. They had also boozed, smoked pot, and chased girls together. But they most often spent their time quietly talking about books and movies and music and life.

In the summer of 1984 Doug joined Katimavik, a federal youth program whereby groups of kids would spend nine months doing volunteer work while travelling around Canada and experiencing communal living. He came back to the Sault telling of the people he'd met, the places he'd seen, and the women he'd fucked. He also showed a greatly increased capacity for drugs and drink. Instead of moving back with his family, Doug found an apartment, and a girl named Amy, who had been in his Katimavik group, came to share it with him.

At this point Tom had graduated from high school but had forsworn going to university. He was still living with his parents and was submitting articles to magazines—he had sold a single short story for thirty-five dollars. He and Doug got on pretty much as they always had: hanging out, listening to tunes, getting drunk and stoned, and, as ever, just rapping.

They both knew Dan Tremblay through Dan's two older brothers, and in the early months of 1986 they were seeing each other pretty regularly, although he was pretty much just an acquaintance. To the older pair Dan was slightly more than someone else's kid brother but not quite a real friend—Doug and Tom would share a few joints with him on occasion and obligingly listen to his theories on existence. Dan himself was doing well in grade ten at Lakeway Collegiate, where he liked to argue with his teachers.

Matt Wright had just arrived at Lakeway from Saint Joseph's Island, a rural area about sixty kilometres east of Sault Ste. Marie. At school Matt and Dan encountered each other without incident, getting together much as Doug and Tom had done years before, exchanging conversation, music, and illicit substances. They were very different in many ways but that didn't seem to matter.

Dan sometimes invited Doug and Tom to little gatherings at his home on Lansdowne Avenue, a ten- or fifteen-minute walk up the hill from Doug's place on Grace Street. It was a good-sized house with a good-sized and very pleasant backyard, and from its second-floor back windows there was an impressive spectacle of the downtown area, as well as the steel plant and the international bridge which connected the Canadian Sault to its same-named American neighbour. The teenaged daughter of a friend of Dan's mother's was staying there—Jeannine was from Espanola and was taking some courses at Lakeway. Tom wanted to lay her and Doug almost did.

Dan and Doug and Tom usually partied in the bright and homely kitchen, sitting around the breakfast table among fresh-picked vegetables, dishes, knick-knacks and cooking utensils (Dan's mom was sensibly tolerant of his toking and drinking). With the approach of summer the setting became even sunnier, even cheerier, and one fine evening Dan had Doug and Tom and Matt all as guests for the first time.

Initially the scene was not good. Dan tried to keep things friendly but Matt's immediate impressions of Tom and Doug, and theirs of him, were unfavorable. Matt was testy and critical of Doug's technique in rolling spliffs, and he dismissed the quality of the hash oil they had bought: "I see you guys got the stuff that's cut with bird seed," he sneered. For their parts Doug and Tom were rather sullen—even in appearance they contrasted with Matt. They always looked like refugees from a Salvation Army sale, and next to them Matt seemed pretty slick with his comparatively short hair and smarter clothes. But as time went on and it became dark outside, the joints were passed and the talk flowed easier, and there was laughter, and tapes were playing on a ghetto blaster and more laughter and the air grew hazy and they were laughing, and somewhere in that kitchen the four freaks started to happen.

*

THE WORD FREAK began to lose its circus sideshow association in the tumultuous late 60s when it was adopted by various sects of the youth underground to apply to any unconventional person; it also became a slangish substitute for "fanatic" or "enthusiast" (hence stereo freak, movie freak, Jesus freak, acid freak and so on). Since that era it had remained in the general language as a designation for all amiable dope-smoking dropouts—hippies and similar creatures. When he was in high school, in fact, Doug had for a time hung out with a crowd of people who were right into the 60s and its historic cultural institutions, for example *Steal This Book*, Woodstock, Vietnam and Revolution. They had called themselves the Freaks.

However, Doug, Tom, Dan and Matt made use of the expression only after they had modified and expanded its meaning. Despite the four freaks' own affinity for the mythic 60s—the Age of Aquarius cast a long shadow over them—a "freak" by their definition did not have to be a living artifact wearing tie-dyes and sporting peace symbols. "Freakness," to them, was something very deep and basic within a person, something that had nothing to do with any superficial, cosmetic identity. They were used to seeing many other young people slot themselves into various classes of preppies, punkers, and headbangers (and this sort of mindless tribalism was by no means a solely adolescent trait), and it both amused and annoyed them when men and women of all ages restrictively defined themselves by their clothes or their music or even by their income or their race or their sex. The most striking characteristic of the freaks was that they had no one striking characteristic. They did not reject the idea of distinct social castes —they turned it back on itself.

Because the four freaks' way of living was such an agreeable mishmash of tastes, interests and attitudes that might have been thought to be irreconcilable, they imagined that non-freaks must surely have been shutting themselves off, limiting themselves. Doug, Tom and Dan once found themselves strolling down Gore Street wearing t-shirts of normally antithetical rock genres: Doug's blared the heavy metal bombast of Iron Maiden, Tom's the classicism of the Beatles, and Dan's the ransom-note rebellion of the Sex Pistols—far out. They could quite literally quote Voltaire while puffing on a joint, and thus they distinguished themselves from Voltaire-quoters who would never smoke pot, or people who did do drugs but who gave no thought to anything so highbrow as French philosophers. Their self-images were focussed on their personalities and their ideologies rather than their hairstyles. The freaks' own, unquestioned, conceit was that their integrity and authenticity removed them from the great herd of people who were naively and shallowly cliquish. The worst epithet in their vocabulary was "trendy"—they had a great distrust of most contemporary, fashionable ideas and customs, and as pleasantly eclectic as their milieu was, it held very few elements that could be considered hip or mid-80s-hot. They saw many people as posers and wannabes, in particular devotees of the New Wave cult, who seemed self-conscious and pretentious in their attempts to appear avant-garde. Ultimately, then, a freak was anyone with (to use criteria that Tom had come up with) a creative mind and an independent spirit. Of course by these standards someone like Adolf Hitler, a sometime watercolour artist with some novel ideas concerning racial hierarchy, could be a freak; to be precise, a freak had a creative mind, an independent spirit, and got into the Stones.

*

THAT SLOW SUMMER of 1986 lingered on easily for the four freaks. Doug, Tom, Dan and Matt got together in no hurry and without effort—it was never planned that they would start hanging out, but increasingly they were spending afternoons and nights and early mornings in each other's company. "Five-bangers" or "fivers" (vials of hash oil weighing five grams) were in luxurious supply: the freaks got stoned often and with an almost spoiled casualness. They went to and fro between their houses and apartments, holding dope and lugging guitars, and they stumbled around the laneways and backstreets of the Sault's forested old inner core. They went out of town, and they stayed in Dan's yard.

Sitting around in the back of Lansdowne Avenue made for some great times. They would lounge out on the picnic table and pass Matt's pipe among them (the pipe was a little carved thing with a native Indian-styled figure on it that could hold rolled joints as well as loose weed) and look up into the galaxy. Or they would romp with Dan's dog Pal, a big, aged mutt who had a little house in the yard—he would play with the freaks for a while before retreating to lie down, certainly fatigued and probably puzzled at the antics of the giggling, Frisbee-tossing stoners. Dan and Tom traded Dan's acoustic guitar back and forth, strumming "Wish

You Were Here," "The Needle and the Damage Done," and "As Tears Go By." In the shimmering daytimes they gazed peacefully out at the endless blue sky, seeing jet contrails and the ethereal moon, and during the lush, luminous nights they devised their own zodiacs from the stars. The backyard became a little haven of fun and relaxation and thoughtful discussions, a sheltered garden away from traffic, crowds, and the city.

The back porch of Doug's apartment on Grace Street was like that too. It was just a small balcony, really, that overlooked a back alley, some decaying houses, and a parking lot, but when the freaks were there they watched the sunsets, drinking beer. Doug and his girlfriend had two cats, Yin and Yang, who enjoyed coming outside to frolic and chase birds. The four freaks preferred partying at the apartment when Amy was out working, as she never really liked Dan and Matt and just tolerated Tom.

The freaks even got out of Sault Ste. Marie for a couple of little excursions that summer. John Keenan, a former Lakeway teacher who Dan knew and admired through his involvement with the local New Democratic Party (Dan fancied himself a diehard left-winger), invited him and Matt up to his cottage north of town for a weekend to do some work, and the pair also found time to swim and canoe and polish off much of a fiver. A while later, Doug and Dan started hitch-hiking to southern Ontario to join up with a commune they had heard about called The Dandelion Project. They were loaded with drugs, and when they could only get as far as North Bay they decided to head back to Whitefish Falls, a community near Manitoulin Island where Dan knew some people. The isolated village was full of unrepentant hippies and other freaks, and Doug and Dan had several days of sunshine, swimming, and smoking dope—they even sampled some opium at one point. They continued their odyssey homeward with baked brains and no money, listening to Creedence Clearwater Revival on the side of the highway on Doug's ghetto blaster. They got some free food at a little restaurant and eventually came back to the Sault exhausted and telling of their adventures.

Still the season shone, drifting through beer and hash oil and guitars and music and lazy good scenes. Dan and Tom spent July 1st, Canada Day, wandering around the waterfront trying to see the fireworks. When they came back to Dan's late that night his mother and Slime gave them hell for making noise and Dan angrily crashed at Tom's. Slime, who answered to the name Bill Richmond, was a sometime radio personality in the Sault and elsewhere in the north, who spoke with the suave, often hungover urbanity of the professional broadcaster while lingering around Lansdowne and corrupting its inhabitants: "That won't do, Dan —that won't do." "So is this good dope, Bill?" "I'm afraid so."

Another time Doug, Dan, Matt, and Dan's brother Joe dropped acid and went up on Collegiate Hill (a scenic lookout below the city's original high school) in the middle of the night, playing guitar, singing Neil Young and freaking out on the view until the cops came and told them to clear out because nearby residents had complained. In those summer months the four freaks found that they got along well enough to keep getting along; they had shared enough dope and enough jokes and enough life to make it seem acceptable to share more. What had begun as an incidental association had started to become a friendship.

*

THE READER MIGHT by now have concluded that the freaks were simply some aimless youths who were proud of the fact that they smoked a lot of marijuana. This would be untrue—Doug, Tom, Dan and Matt were actually about as skeptical of drugs and alcohol as they were about most everything else, and they definitely had no illusions as to their intoxicants' harmfulness: "Shall we inhale some carcinogens?" Matt would suggest as he rolled up a joint. Dope and drink were no more or less enjoyable than a hot cup of Dan's tea or Doug's coffee, no more essential to their lives than good conversation or good tunes—but they did take much more effort and money to obtain, which made the stuff seem much more valuable to the four freaks than it actually was.

This is not to say that their substance abuse never reached excessive or dangerous levels, because at times all four put away amounts that could not be considered prudent. Yet they managed to avoid developing truly serious habits, even if they did show some mental and physical wear and tear. The hardest drug they ever took was acid (cocaine was available in the Sault but they never went looking for it), although Tom abstained from the chemical and, he being the most conscientious of the group, would abstain from all other stuff for short periods as well: "fasts," he called them. Nor did the others ever encourage him or themselves to do any more than they already were doing—"peer pressure" was unknown to the freaks. The strength of their personalities and that down-to-earth skepticism helped them avoid the pitfalls that so many simple, white-bread, characterless suburbanites had not. And, of course, the unreliable nature of the local drug trade was an automatic retardant of heavy intakes, as the not infrequent weeks when dope became scarce—for whatever reason—meant that they would temporarily all have to go cold turkey (or cool turkey, at least). In the end, their vices were always the background against which the other concerns of their lives were played out. The story of the four freaks is not a story of liquor and drugs but of people who happened to consume them.

*

THE ONSET of fall brought many changes. Each freak was finding more and more that he had only the others to turn to for camaraderie: Doug's Amy had moved back to her home in Halifax (Doug was to join her in a month or two); two close friends of Tom, Chris Bradshaw and Dan Duggan, had left for college and university in Brampton and Ottawa; and when Dan and Matt went back to Lakeway (which was to close down the following June) the school seemed fuller of trendies, jocks, and general assholes than ever. Although the two students made a few friends and girlfriends there, and had homework and other projects to do, and although they kept up with gossip and goings-on, they gave little thought to the whole high school scene. For Dan and Matt, and for Doug and Tom, the freak trip became the focus of their social lives.

Doug and the two cats moved out of the apartment and back to his parents' place on Woodward Avenue. He was understandably reluctant in this, but he could not live alone on his income from Unemployment Insurance, and anyway, he hoped to be down east in a short time. He and the other three emptied the place on Grace Street, reminiscing silently to themselves as they carried the household away in boxes and tossed the twin mattress over the balcony, leaving it for junk.

Tom was feeling in a rut as he prepared to spend another year trying to write and trying to work on his Super-8 films. He wasn't accomplishing a lot and his biggest achievements appeared to be figuring out songs on his guitar and spending Wednesday afternoons in the public library, leafing through magazines as he wondered how much more stagnant his life would become.

Matt and Dan, both frustrated with their situations at home, briefly shared a place near the end of summer. They stayed at the apartment on Huron Street a single week, but while Dan moved back up the hill to face the worsening interrelationship of his mother, Slime and himself, Matt's taste of independent living led him to a new pad—he would take the third floor of a house at a busy intersection near the railway tracks, directly across from the Blue Boy restaurant. From the side that faced out to John Street the building looked like not a bad old place, but around the back it resembled a tenement, a shabby slab of bricks stuck beside the rear of a crumbling shoe store, rising up from a barren gravel parking lot. Roosting pigeons and a spindly steel staircase completed the ghetto image. Inside it was a nice size, consisting of a main living room-bedroom-kitchen, as well as a small spare room and a bathroom, but the windows were small and the already dark interior became genuinely gloomy in the weak light. Matt made the most of the apartment, however: he covered the walls liberally with rock posters and other artwork, and the appliances and furniture he brought in (some courtesy of Doug) also lessened the attic-like aura. He would live on welfare since he still had his schooling to attend to; throughout autumn his residence was frequently visited by Dan and Doug and Tom.

The four freaks spent many nights there, huddled around the

small red table in the corner beneath the sloping ceiling, slapping cassettes in the portable stereo and dragging on joints. The oily days of summer were gone—Sault Ste. Marie was entering a dry period for drugs ("Operation Blitz," a series of much-publicized police raids in the summer, was having an effect), and the freaks were having difficulty finding a regular dealer or a constant supply of reliable dope. They mostly smoked grass in those times, if they could find it.

A typical get-together of that era would start off with Tom leaving his house near the hospitals and travelling a couple of blocks to pick up Doug; then they would bicycle up the hill through a maze of backstreets until they came to Dan's. Tom's bike is worth a note: it was a broken-down three-speed that his father had ridden more than ten years earlier—Tom got it in rusty, rideable condition again, painted it solid black and put "BLACK PLAGUE" on it in white transfer letters. He also installed a light on the rear forks, in a predictable concession to law and order. The Plague, as the guys came to call it, was rickety and temperamental ("Fuckin' thing's a deathtrap," Matt said after taking a spin), but it was fast and Tom got a lot of bone-rattling use out of it.

After hanging out at Lansdowne for a bit the three would take another roundabout westward tour through side streets, enter the short alley into the parking lot behind Matt's, and then take the cold bare flights of steps up to the door where their unsmiling host would let them in. They would pass hours with music and arguments and what always seemed to be the last of someone's stash, sitting in the shadows as the black-and-white TV flickered silently. Sometimes it got chilly and Matt would open the bathroom door and turn the shower on hot, his rough-and-ready method of heating the place up. Doug and Tom were learning to interpret Matt's sour ravings as his means of expression, so when he now barked "*Fuck off!*" in their faces they knew he was just being friendly.

Dan often ended up crashing at Matt's, but Tom and Doug usually unlocked their wheels and rode home along the waterfront. It was a long and pleasant route—in the late hours they never encountered much traffic—and as they sped into the wind and the rain and the leaves, bundled up against the sharp October or November air, yawing across the roads, they were sort of earthbound fighter pilots, racing alone against the vast night. Meanwhile the other two would still be seated near the lamp on the red table, Dan optimistically chirping about this and that, Matt disdainful as usual. The ominous, sombre seasonal dark crept and cut into the four freaks' world, yet they kept convening through the days and the weeks, keeping warm in Matt's apartment.

One time, Tom and Doug got a twenty-sixer of Jack Daniel's with money Tom had earned mowing lawns and shared it with Dan in his bedroom at Lansdowne. When they started heading down to Matt's it was obvious Dan was very, very drunk—he was insensible as Doug doubled him down the steep hill on his bike, and later he unzipped and took a piss in the middle of a sedate neighbourhood, declaring "I'm the new Abbie Hoffman," while his two friends laughed and shook their heads. Further on, as he staggered merrily across people's yards, Dan became mushy as only inebriates can: "I love you guys, I love you guys…You guys are my buddies," he was saying, and when they were finally at their destination he cuddled up to Matt (not a cuddler himself), and blathered, "Oh, buddy, I love you man... You guys are my buddies ... I love you, buddy," over and over.

"Fuck off, willya, you fuckin' lush," Matt snarled, and then asked the relatively sober Doug and Tom, "Jesus, how much did you guys drink?" It looked as if Dan was about to pass out until Matt produced a little bit of oil he had left, whereupon he stabilized himself long enough to smoke some, and after that he really did pass out. Down on Matt's mattress, he dribbled out vomit as the others worried about him "pulling a Bonham," referring to Led Zeppelin's late drummer John Bonham, who had choked to death on his own puke under similarly annihilated circumstances. Eventually they gave up on him, leaving him to either be sick, sleep, or pull a Bonham on his own. It wasn't the first time Dan had boozed himself out cold, nor would it be the last.

From his parents' house Doug had been making arrangements with Amy via long distance phone calls, and he had already sent several packages of his things out to her on the east coast. But with every communication they grew uneasy about their futures with each other—the rollercoaster of ups and downs they'd been through while they had lived together was fresh in their memories, and they wondered if it was worth making another go of it. Twice Doug was ready to fly out to Halifax to settle their problems; twice he held back and thought the scene over. Finally he and Amy mutually agreed to stay apart and reclaim their separate selves. His stuff was sent back up to the Sault, and, in a kind of custody deal, she would get Yin, the frisky female cat they had shared, and he would keep male Yang, the larger animal, solid black, whose calmly enigmatic poise matched his own.

An old chum of Doug's named Dan Larocque had been in

contact with him and raised the idea of the two jointly getting an apartment, now that Doug would be staying in town for the next few months at minimum. It sounded good, and by the first of December they were moving into a place on Blucher Street, a short strip of homes right downtown, roughly halfway between Dan's and Matt's. It was no mansion—in fact the two-storey building didn't even appear to be completed, as the dull yellow outside was woefully bare of shingles or other covering, and a child's swing set rusting in the front yard stood as one of its few signs of regular habitation. The upper floor, which Doug and Larocque would occupy, was unappealing: at the top of the stairs the visitor was confronted by walls and a confining hallway which linked the kitchen, the can, the two bedrooms and a box-like chamber at the front which would do as a living room. They put up posters of bands, demons, skeletons riding motorcycles and other freaky pictures, but these hardly diminished the setup's claustrophobic limitations.

The four freaks now got together often at this new pad, although Matt's was still a hangout and Dan's had not been entirely abandoned. (They hardly ever partied at Tom's—sometimes they would blow a furtive joint or two in his room, or watch late movies or listen to tunes, but the house was seldom the site of a full-fledged freak bash.) Unfortunately, the aforementioned living room was cramped and cursed with a cold bright light that was inappropriate for being stoned beneath, and besides the stereo and records there was only space enough for stiff, upright chairs placed closely around an equally upright square table, the kind that usually has a large umbrella sprouting from its centre. It was all quite severe and quite inimical to partying, having neither the charm of Dan's kitchen nor the mellowness of Matt's apartment. Nevertheless Doug, Tom, Dan and Matt assembled there regularly into the new year, hearing the chants emanating from the Indian Friendship Centre, a Native meeting hall on the corner of Blucher Street, as the pagan songs whirled with the winter wind outside the windows. "Fuckin' trippy," Doug said after the ceremonies died down and they resumed their own. Awkward as it was, lots of dope was smoked beneath the glare, and the freaks did not complain when they were enjoying themselves. As a blasted Tom remarked, in imitation of Fred Flintstone's robotic duplicates recalled from the cartoon series, "*Yabba…dabba…do!*" Good, squalid, stupid, times.

It wasn't until the early weeks of 1987 when Doug's landlord enlisted his help for a few days to do some renovation—knocking down walls and such—that the place was opened up and rearranged into a decidedly more pleasing configuration. The living room would become Doug's sleeping quarters, and Larocque's bedroom, by enlarging the window and removing the partition, was cleared out to become the new living room, or what would become known as the Jive Hive.

The landlord, who lived downstairs, was a young guy by the name of Clay Johnstone. He was bearish and likeable, and his arms were tattooed extensively—he looked like one of the less dangerous members of a motorcycle gang, for although he didn't own a hog he knew a lot of people who did, and he also was usually supplied with a particularly vicious grade of hash oil that he didn't mind selling to his tenants and their friends. The freaks found this wonderfully convenient, and he became a regular visitor at Doug's apartment, passing thickly laden joints around and chuckling a lot. He was a family man: his two little kids sometimes came up while he was partying and he would lovingly sit them on his knee and be paternal even as the air was filled with sweet mind-expanding smoke.

*

TOLERANT AND JOLLY, Clay was one of an assortment of people who were fixtures of the four freaks' world. Doug, Tom, Dan and Matt by no means considered themselves an exclusive club, and they welcomed many individuals into the freak "family," a crew of relations, friends and familiars who populated and hugely enriched their scene.

Doug's roommate Dan Larocque had a job with Budget Rent-a-Car, shuttling vehicles from the airport to town and back, so he was never at home much ("How was your day, dear?" Doug would ask when Larocque came back to the apartment in the evenings). He also had a girlfriend who lived in the west end, and he stayed at her place quite a bit, which also kept him away from Blucher. Doug was a little disappointed to see that Larocque, with whom he used to get stoned and shoot cars with BB guns, was now straighter and more reserved than he'd been in the past—Doug would admit that, to him, "Anyone with a *job* is a yuppie," but poor Larocque, with his dress shirts and his ties and his newfound sense of responsibility, was as yuppie as the four freaks would ever care to be.

The term Jive Hive, which soon became the nickname for the new parlour of Doug's apartment, was coined by Chris Bradshaw, a smart, funny freak who went way back with Doug and Tom. Among years and years of shared escapades they had inhaled great amounts of his smoke and been audience to his cosmic discourses on history, religion, physics, and acid trips. Chris, a talented painter and musician, was at present down at art college in southern Ontario, but he came back up north every so often and customarily stopped in to see the boys. Previously, in the summer of 1986, he'd got stoned with Doug, Tom and Dan once while Doug was house-sitting for his vacationing parents, and he spent most of the evening in hysterics, pounding on the kitchen table and crying "*More, more!*" He was right on.

So was Glen Crane, the virtuoso guitar player who formed a band with Matt called Lone Faith (Matt was the singer). Glen and Matt had known each other for some time, and though Lone Faith broke up after playing only a couple of gigs at a local youth club—actually not such a bad track record, considering most other garage bands never get to perform publicly at all—the former metal god of Thessalon, Ontario stayed around and got to know all the freaks. His big musical inspirations were Ace Frehley of Kiss, and Randy Rhoads, who was with Ozzy Osbourne before dying in a plane crash, but he could also do accurate versions of Hank Williams Jr.'s "A Country Boy Can Survive," David Bowie's "Rebel Rebel," and Stevie Ray Vaughan's "Look At Little Sister." He had a massive Peavey amplifier that was the envy of Tom and Dan and the despair of many a downstairs neighbour. Apart from his skill as an axeman, Glen's low-keyed drollery ("Right on, heavy, *and* solid") made him a favourite among the guys.

By the end of winter Doug was sick of doing nothing while living on Unemployment, and so he joined Futures, another in a long line of government-sponsored plans designed to assist young people in finding careers and gaining job experience. In his mind it was little more than make-work bullshit, but it was money and better than staring at the walls, and he found that most of the others who daily went to the office-classroom with him were similarly motivated. One of them was Raymond "Ray" Deneault, who started hanging out with Doug and the other freaks and ended up as one of the regulars of their scene. In his early twenties, he was even more of a lowlife than they were: he'd been in and out of jail (he was living in a seedy hotel when Doug met him) and he still had a hobby of thieving money and other stuff (he burned a guy's jacket out of a truck and he and Doug wondered if and how they could use the bank cards they found in it); he still had some drug-trafficking charges coming up; he got into high-decibel thrash metal and he was always challenging the others to arm-wrestling matches. He claimed to have once finished a fiver with a couple of other guys in one sitting—"We were burnt for three days," was his recollection. His badass biography made the four freaks appear practically uptight, but notwithstanding this, and the fact that he wasn't the brightest bulb around, Ray was accepted by them and added a shadier dimension to their state of being, which was disreputable as it stood.

Then there was Rick Jones, a rangy, hawknosed dude with a taste for slasher movies, rye whiskey and country music, who Tom and Doug first knew working at a small used book store that they had shopped at for ages. Only recently, however, had they and the others acquainted themselves with him (he even turned out to be a cousin of Matt's, though the two had hardly seen each other since they'd been children), and once they did he became a close friend of them all. Parallelling Deneault, Rick had been in trouble with the cops—he was on probation awaiting trials for possessing dope and break-and-enter tools, and he had a court-imposed curfew—but this belied his refinement and his knack for sly, laconic teasing. He took in a lot of books and films and he enjoyed talking for hours about anything heavy, and as much as the freaks were happy to have him around, he seemed even happier to get into their trip, where his literacy and cultivation were not just permitted but greeted as qualities of a kindred spirit.

Joe.

Joe, Joe, Joe, Joe.

Joseph Gordon Paul Tremblay, the oldest of the Tremblay brothers, was unquestionably the most extraordinary of the four freaks' associates—but then, he was probably the most extraordinary associate of nearly everyone who ever met him. Doug, Tom, Dan and Matt and their other friends might have been odd; Joe was unreal. He was always a singular phenomenon, defying comparisons or classification: once you got to know him, you didn't mistake Joe for anyone else.

As a visual experience alone, he was outrageous. His posture maintained a perpetual tottering droop, as if his whole frame was about to collapse in on itself. He was topped with a great pile of dark brown hair that was almost Afro-styled, and he also had an irregular, scraggly goatee. His eyes were big, blue, and bulgy, and mostly half-open (even when he slept); he had a classically large nose, full lips, and grey teeth; his face was altogether sallow. Joe often wore sunglasses, even in receding daylight—either square dark ones or a round purple-shaded pair, and the rest of his costume was as curious, consisting of clothes that could once have been dressy in a quirky way (dress shirts, corduroy pants, occasionally moccasins, and a long woolen overcoat), but which clad him as drab castoffs. The other freaks were certainly scruffy, but Joe, in short, looked like a hobo.

Appearances aside, he still presented himself with formidable weirdness. In his temperament he dwelt in the shadowy province between extreme eccentricity and mild mental illness—his speech was slow and rambling and often incoherent, full of mumbled metaphors (*"The key is in the lock and it's not comin' out"*) and misplaced quotes from Bob Dylan songs (Dylan was his idol, and indeed Joe bore a strong resemblance to the folk-rock superstar), and the baffling monologues were always conducted as he sighed and spun his eyes and chain-smoked "rollioes" (hand-rolled cigarettes, invariably stuffed with Drum tobacco, fired by matches which he never, ever lit with less than three strikes). One encounter with the guy would convince anyone of his peculiarity, at least, but remember the four freaks (Dan most of all, obviously) had been encountering Joe for a long, long time.

Tom and Doug had first known him at Alex Muir, where he hadn't been any less strange than his current self, other than clean-shaven. At age eleven Tom was called by his mother to see what she called "a clown" outside the house, which turned out to be the adolescent Joe walking down the street wearing self-applied Kiss makeup and an expression of fearless what-are-you-looking-at dignity. "That's no clown, Mom," said Tom, "that's Joe Tremblay."

They did not see him a lot for a period after that, as he went on to a different high school, and then left town to stay with his dad in Alberta—"Acid was quite plentiful out there," Joe later recalled. He returned to the Sault in 1984, and he and his two old classmates, and Dan too, had fraternized a great deal, in the typical freak way: playing music, drinking, smoking dope ("Sorting out some personal problems," Joe explained to a snooping straight when they were getting high down by the docks), and getting into concepts. But then Joe found a girlfriend, if such a positive word could describe her. Mary, easily ten years older than him, was a wan, wasted woman who had survived two suicide attempts and a number of placements in mental hospitals; she looked frail and undernourished, and the paradox of the romance was that if neither of them seemed any good for each other, they were sort of evenly matched, a psychotic's vision of young love. "I thought the groom's name was Zimmerman," Doug and Tom overheard someone say at the inevitable wedding, and they smirked helplessly at the idea of Joe's deranged obsession with Bob Dylan, true name Robert Zimmerman. Even as he was getting married, he would not display any signal of being completely sound-minded.

After his nuptials in September of 1985, Joe became a semi-legendary figure, often spoken of but rarely seen. By the time Doug, Tom, Dan and Matt were getting together he was an abstraction—they saw him recurrently but they couldn't make any sense of his life and they knew it would be foolish to try. His marriage to Mary was a disaster, of course; they split up and got back together, split up and got back together, off and on and on and off until not even they seemed to know or care about the state of their relationship. She tried to kill herself again, and still she and her husband carried on their bizarre alliance, living with and without each other, having violent fights that left ugly gouges on his forearms, spiralling into a ruinous matrimonial vortex. Since moving out of Lansdowne Joe had lived in no less than eleven places in and around Sault Ste. Marie, some shared with Mary, some not, all of them dingy and reeking of pot, stale food, and cat shit—if Doug's Jive Hive was usually untidy, these abodes were mainly unhealthy (Tom: "Fuckin' place sure smells, eh?" Doug: "It doesn't smell, it tastes."). He lived on welfare, being what bureaucrats call "chronically unemployed." A couple of times he got into trouble with the cops for not paying his rent, and he was roughed up by the son of one of his landlords for leaving an apartment in disrepair. He was even beaten and ripped off while trying to score a fiver.

Sitting around Doug's place, Dan would ask, "Has Joe surfaced lately?" That was a good way to put it, for his brother lived in a perpetually murky, subterranean environment, whose only other denizens seemed to be very wrecked human beings like Mary, or his friend Tony, a fortyish, English-accented fellow who was a total and utter alcoholic—he went through bottles of rum from hour to hour, and when asked a question it took him some time to comprehend it before he slurred a reply from the pit of what was left of his brain. There was a chilling air of futility about Joe's life: "Oh, Joe has his shit together," Dan would say loyally, and Matt would grimace as he scoffed, "Joe doesn't have his shit together...You ever see that guy staggerin' around at four-thirty in the morning?" It did look as if he was fucked; so were all the freaks in one way or another, to be sure, but with Joe being fucked was less a description than a diagnosis.

And yet, as difficult as he was to respect, he was more difficult to dislike. Sometimes, after the four freaks had rapped disgustedly about his latest fuckup and his gift for digging ever deeper holes for himself, they would lean back and relent somewhat, and Doug might lighten up and say, "Yeah, but...Joe's great." He *was* great—it was a warped and demented sort of greatness, but it was greatness all the same. And though it was awkward to think of Joe, in his sad condition, as a freak, it was also endearing and uplifting.

He did piss them off at times, not just because of the sorry persistence with which he spoiled his own scenes but, as well, because of his habit of spoiling theirs: he'd owed Tom fifty bucks for almost two years ("Oh, don't worry, dude, you'll definitely get your money"), he still had a bunch of his stuff taking up space in Matt's apartment (Matt had actually picked the pad up when Joe and Mary moved out), and Doug noticed his cassettes and other small items tended to go missing after Joe paid him a visit—the guy had seriously light fingers. But for all that, he was overwhelmingly winning, in his incurable optimism; in his endless get-rich-quick schemes to organize a radio station or a bar or a recording studio; in his composing off-beat, Dylanesque (what else?) poetry; in his shuffling, stumbling walk that verged on being a limp; in his always complaining of assorted ailments and fatigue—"I'm runnin' on fumes..."; in his unpredictable custom of banging on Doug's or Matt's doors in the wee hours, holding some really wild dope and wanting to share it; in his surprised, startled, bewildered reactions to being hailed on the street; in his happy-go-lucky eagerness to sample whatever drugs he could steal from the mental ward of the hospital, his wife's ostensible second home; in his accommodating, carefree, inexplicably cheery soul. Joe really was one of them, and to Doug, Tom, Dan and Matt he could perhaps even be called the "fifth freak," a kind of wayward cousin who'd fallen on hard times. They felt for him and they could not forget him. No one ever could.

*

THE JIVE HIVE had quickly established itself as the freaks' headquarters. It was the perfect combination of snug comfort and intimate informality, and served as both the bustling central hub of the whole scene during the day—it was where people went to find out what was going down, for sooner or later everyone could be met there—and a private oasis of fun times long into the night. The layout could not have been improved upon, since every element seemed flawless and flawlessly placed, from the large low circular coffee table (borrowed from Joe), which was surrounded by the sofa, some shelves of paperbacks, a plush easy chair, another couple of seats, and the all-important stereo and TV cabinet, to the big westward-facing window and the big mirror on the adjacent wall, which together lit the entire room wonderfully. It was an ideal locale.

As a place to get stoned the Jive Hive was second only to oriental opium dens in its tranquil, decadent coziness. Lying on the couch one could trip and stare out at the setting sun, as the majestically billowing smoke from the steel plant added to the spacey light show; at your left you could choose from Doug's diverse selection of books—he owned an anthology of Gustave Doré's drawings from *The Divine Comedy*, and everyone liked to buzz out on *Castles*, a sumptuously illustrated volume of medieval lore; then there were handy piles of records and tapes to play; or you could just lean over the table and fire up a bottle toke. Bottle tokers, or BTers, were quaint but extremely useful pieces of drug paraphernalia: by breaking a little hole at the base of an empty bottle, a lighted cigarette with a dab of hash oil on the burner could be inserted, and the oil would go up in a dense cloud that could then be gulped through the bottle's mouth. No freak scene was complete without a BTer, and although the freaks did not invent the device they turned them into a kind of folk art by regarding them as more than merely tools—they chose bottles with an eye to their aesthetic properties, and Doug even emblazoned an exotic, occult painting on his.

And oil was, without a doubt, the four freaks' dope of choice—not that they were choosy. The thick, dark, cannabis-derived resin was harsh and inelegant and not for the faint of heart, being to good weed what backwoods moonshine is to fine champagne; it bore into one's brain with all the subtlety of a vaporous jackhammer and left even the hardiest of souls feeling as if their cerebra were soggy with warm wet cement. As Matt put it, "Grass gets you high, but oil gets you stoned." Just before unleashing a bombardment of oil-smeared joints on Tom, Doug had bluntly warned, "I'm gonna smoke you into the ground," and he'd picked the right shit to do it with.

Tunes were another component of the freak scene. The sound system didn't matter (and they never did own really good ones)—what mattered was the music, and the expansive variety of artists they got into strikingly illustrated their reflective and discriminating tastes: albums of both Ronnie James Dio and Ray Charles sat next to each other in Doug's record bin, and Tom's collection contained the Everly Brothers and Led Zeppelin. Janis Joplin might follow the Police into Matt's ghetto blaster, and Dan's turntable spun Pink Floyd as well as Buddy Holly. Theirs was an idiosyncratic repertoire, Dan and Tom freaking out on some Russian folk music and Doug and Matt elsewhere blasting heavy metal; they always came back, though, to solid late 60s-early 70s rock 'n' roll: the Beatles, the Rolling Stones, Led Zeppelin, Pink Floyd, David Bowie, Neil Young, Blue Öyster Cult, Black Sabbath, AC/DC, Alice Cooper, Jethro Tull, Fleetwood Mac, Cat Stevens, Nazareth, Bob Dylan, Jimi Hendrix,

Creedence Clearwater Revival, Aerosmith, Janis Joplin, and especially T-Rex, whose incongruous blend of engagingly whimsical lyrics and roaring power chords neatly fit their own sensibilities.

Most of these, admittedly, were among the most famous and successful rock 'n' rollers ever, hardly corresponding with the four freaks' self-declared nonconformity. But by 1987 nearly all this music was quite out-of-date, and even some albums that had topped the charts in years past were now hard to find or totally out of print, or existing only as sonic memorabilia for nostalgic yuppies. Insofar as they listened to these tunes all the time as living, breathing material, it was rare music indeed. Post-1979 records were not commonly heard in their places, for they felt that most contemporary pop was synthetic and force-fed to them, and they also distrusted the recent efforts of once-greats like Bruce Springsteen or David Bowie or the Stones. Moreover, the actual songs they did listen to were usually lesser-known pieces that had never been popular radio fodder—certainly not in Sault Ste. Marie—and Doug, Tom, Dan and Matt consequently devised an unofficial Top Ten, as from week to week and month to month little gems became big hits with them: Pink Floyd's thundering "The Nile Song," say, and the Stones' sixteen-cylinder "Bitch," Jimi Hendrix's mind-blowing "All Along the Watchtower" and "The Wind Cries Mary," as well as Black Sabbath's apocalyptic "Warning" (featuring the droning voice of a pre-horror-makeup, pre-bird-biting Ozzy Osbourne), and the Beatles' "I Want You (She's So Heavy)" which highlighted an acid party at Doug's on Grace Street.

Led Zeppelin struck hard with "The Rover" and "Trampled

Underfoot," from *Physical Graffiti*; "Winterlong" and "Deep Forbidden Lake" by Neil Young went down heavily, as did Jethro Tull's far-out "Locomotive Breath," Bob Seger's "Rock 'n' Roll Never Forgets," CCR's "Lodi," and Nazareth's "Razamanaz." Some of the harder stuff included "Holy Diver" by Dio (Doug's metal favourites), "The Temples of Syrinx" by Rush, Judas Priest's "Victim of Changes" from *Sad Wings of Destiny*, and "Is It My Body," by the king of shock rock, Alice Cooper. Pink Floyd's titanic slab of psychedelia, "Time," was blasted frequently, and Dan used to listen to their "Echoes" on his walkman while drifting home on the railway tracks, stoned out of his head in the dead of winter in the dead of night, at some risk to his sanity; David Bowie's "Changes," "Oh! You Pretty Things," and "Panic in Detroit" were extremely cool; likewise "Heaven" and "Tops," the Rolling Stones' sensuous soul songs from *Tattoo You*, and Matt turned the others on to AC/DC by way of "Little Lover" ("Severe blues attack"—Dan) and "TNT," from *High Voltage*.

Janis Joplin's "Summertime" and "Down on Me" made an impact on the freaks, and the Beatles' "Everybody's Got Something to Hide Except for Me and My Monkey" did too. "Jeepster" and "Telegram Sam" by T. Rex were always being played; so was Bob Marley's "No Woman No Cry," and Tom and Dan blew out to more Beatles, namely "Rain" and "Tomorrow Never Knows." The two also spent an evening getting drunk and playing the Stones' singalong "Salt of the Earth," and when Matt and Glen in Lone Faith covered "2000 Man," again by the Stones, everyone else got into it. And the mighty Zeppelin made another raid with the beautiful "Tangerine" and the sweeping blues of "Since I've Been Loving You." All of this freak rock used to fill the Jive Hive as the freaks closed around the stereo or the blaster, absorbing the sounds like heat from the glowing embers of a bonfire.

*

AMIDST THE PUNGENT smog of fuming hash oil and the sludgy strains of Black Sabbath it is easy to overlook the freaks' not inconsiderable intelligence. At the very least it could be said that their more cretinous conduct and conversation (Matt's eerie intoning of Satanic gibberish, for instance, or Tom's oh-wow-is-that-ever-heavy responses to soap bubbles and other profundities) was always partly tongue-in-cheek—they would sort of nudge themselves whenever they enacted the clichés of the stoner hoodlum lifestyle, or when they started sounding like an old Cheech and Chong or McKenzie Brothers comedy tape.

But further than this, Doug, Tom, Dan and Matt were actually quite cultured people who read novels and poetry, and who painted and drew and who wrote songs and stories and verses of their own. They weren't brilliant intellectuals, but nor were they illiterate morons. Dan read Dickens and Camus and Joyce and Ayn Rand and science fiction. Doug had just finished John Fowles' *The Magus*, and his bookshelves were crammed with well-thumbed works of Dante, Plato, Hesse, Orwell, Tom Wolfe, Harlan Ellison, Ken Kesey, Stephen King, and a thousand trashy bestsellers. Fantasy and art volumes were Matt's main reads, while Tom held out for F. Scott Fitzgerald, Antoine de Saint Exupéry, and histories, biographies, and criticism. They were always trading and recommending and debating literature, and occasionally they would even make a book the focus of a party, passing it around and getting off on it like a joint—*Castles* was good for this, as was *A Child's Garden of Grass*, a dead-on, hilarious manual of pot use:

under the heading "Hiding places to avoid," the suggestion "Throwing it way up high" was listed—"Excellent, for very short periods of time."

The four freaks created, too. Doug and Tom and Matt each had a talent for drawing and illustrating: during get-togethers they filled sketch pads with symbols, logos, and doodles of demons and guitars and women and other wild shit, and added to this they came out with large-scale finished productions depicting more women, more rock stars, and more mystical imagery. Dan and Matt used to make sizable collages of clippings from books and magazines. One was a scathing political satire that featured a photo of Prime Minister Brian Mulroney shaking hands with President Ronald Reagan, under which the headline "A Sordid Sex Life at the Top" was placed. They also did a big and very iconic one of the Beatles. And all the freaks wrote songs, poems, and stories—Tom's "The Preacher Behind the Wall," a grotesque horror yarn, had been published in a small magazine, and Doug had written a complete novel called *Earth Cowboy*, about a rebel disc jockey and his influence on a gang of listless small-town down-and-outers; it was a pensive, troubling tale that ended in suicide and disillusionment. Few, if any, of the freaks' artistic compositions could be called works of genius, but their being artistic at all was a noteworthy counterpoint to their less redeeming pursuits.

*

THE SLEETY GREYNESS of winter's final weeks weighed down on each of them, in some ways that were merely bothersome and in others that were more cruel. Dan's and Tom's glasses fogged up every time they came in from the cold. Matt was shivering inside his apartment. Tom kept making his deathly quiet treks home at 2:45 in the frozen still mornings. And Doug had stayed like a cave-dweller in the Jive Hive, smoking oil all day, growing ashen-faced and spiritless. When at last they warily emerged out onto the streets, dust in the wind and dry, to bask in the rays of the unfamiliar yellow star that had been hidden for so long, it was not so much a time of hope as a time of relief.

Now things started to pick up a little, if not in quality then in variety—Doug got into Futures, and Ray Deneault was making his initial visits; so was Rick Jones. Rick and Tom were pleased to meet each other and find that they both had great interests in the cinema, not just as moviegoers but as aspiring movie makers, and they had long raps about films and directors and their respective show business dreams. But of all the new developments of that cold, sunny season, the most significant was Matt's moving out of his pad by the Blue Boy and into a new place on Blucher Street, just across from Doug's. Apart from being roomier and more liveable, its proximity to the Jive Hive centralized the freak scene and eased problems of distance and communication: Doug and Matt had never had phones in their residences, so finding either of them at home was largely a hit-or-miss affair, but now that they were so close (from Matt's third floor window you could look across into Doug's living room and spy on its stoned occupants) they and the others could stay in contact without roving all over downtown. The heyday of the four freaks was at hand.

Deneault had been crashing at the Jive Hive (Larocque was scarcely there two days out of the week; a few times he had partied with the guys and dazedly played Chinese Checkers), but with his income from Futures he reasoned he could move in with Matt and

Matt said it was okay. Their apartment became a kind of annex of Doug's, as the freaks often casually traversed between the two: this inaugurated the era of the "Blucher Boys," a lively period of spontaneous parties and impromptu droppings-in that reaffirmed the Jive Hive's status as the heart of freakdom.

They came and went offhandedly—Doug took the bull by the horns and had a telephone installed, and then Matt was over daily, calling his girlfriend who lived in the east end. It was not even that unusual for Doug to leave Dan or Tom there while he and Matt or Rick or Deneault went to score from any of the half-dozen or so regular and irregular dealers who were known to them. These were mostly jobless young men like themselves, idling around the one-room apartments and pool halls of downtown Sault Ste. Marie. "Hey McGyver, wanna buy a fiver?" was the come-on of one familiar. Others were surly strangers who lived a low-rent version of *Scarface*, like the Ojibway heavies who told Dan and Glen Crane they still owed another twenty on a vial they'd just bought. "You don't leave until you pay," threatened one guy. Dead silence. "For what?" "Fer yer *bullshit*." Somehow the surcharges were avoided, and Dan and Glen backed out uneasily.

By the springtime dope was once again hard to find, since more busts had gone down—Clay's supplier had been nabbed—and while they vigorously sought a good connection there were long stretches when nobody could get a hold of anything. "Is anything happening there?" they'd ask over the phone, and a flat voice on the other end would answer, "Fuck-all." Click. The atmosphere during these famines was like that of a forgotten outpost town awaiting some kind of salvation that never arrived, rife with rumours and speculation that remained rumours and speculation: "I hear there's oil in the west end." "Kaszycki's s'posed to be sellin' grams." "Yeah, we should be gettin' a visit from 'Uncle Sidney' pretty soon." "I might have a line on a QP." "QP?" "Quarter pound." "They say there'll be a big shipment in any day now." "Shit, they've been sayin' that for fuckin' three weeks." They say, I heard, they say, I heard.

In general terms, of course, the four freaks had drugs more than they didn't have them, indeed to such an extent that they could be heard referring to themselves with bitter self-mockery as burnouts or addicts. But that was overstating it, for though they did get a bit frazzled, they lacked the permanent lifeless dementia that was the mark of the truly charred. And along with evading the greater drawbacks of dope use, they had indeed discovered that pot seemed to have its benefits—not as an anaesthetic to help them cope with society's pressures, as the uninformed always insisted, but as a bridge to a pleasant state of hyper-awareness, a means by which one could temporarily alter one's consciousness. It was more of a sacrament than a sedative.

Neither marijuana nor acid are Jekyll-and-Hyde drugs, because for the stoner there is a very grey area where normal thought patterns end and genuinely fucked-up thinking begins, and while most stoned observations (sensory or conceptual) are very trivial or very obscure, they are rarely crazy or meaningless. Witness Tom's compiling of "funny sayings": after sucking back several BTs, he would often be struck by some remark that one of the others had made and, giggling, scramble about for a pen and a scrap of paper to write it down. Hours afterward, upon getting home and coming down hard, he would reread the phrase in the light of his bedside lamp, and to his red-eyed wonder he found that it would be as comical when he was straight as when he was gunned out of his head. For all the liabilities of smoking up and tripping out, then, Doug, Tom, Dan and Matt were usually able to harness the effects of dope into positive forces that fired their imaginations without frying their psyches.

Even with the clamour of activity on and around Blucher Street, the Jive Hive maintained its basic peacefulness. Whatever else was going down, the room had an almost hypnotic power to settle people, to mellow them out. It wasn't just the BTs or the booze, or the music or the books—it was the pristine *righteousness* of it all, in the communal glass of water that always sat conveniently on the table (bottle tokes were pretty hard on the larynx), in the wide wall-hanging that reproduced a poster from *Easyriders* magazine, showing a biker on his Harley riding even with the ghost of an old-time outlaw on his horse. Doug sometimes lit candles there—one night he put one in the window and Matt, across the street, responded with some of his own, making a pair of spooky, flickering beacons—which heightened the restful isolation of the scene. Dan was never bothered by Slime there; Matt did not have to pay rent or other bills to lie back on the couch. The Jive Hive was far away from the windswept grounds of the bus terminal where Tom would catch last rides home at 12:30 a.m., and the Jive Hive was where Doug could talk and joke with his friends and not be so isolated, so withdrawn, and so alone.

*

THE FREAKS were perhaps not quite as mature or experienced as they liked to think they were—none of them had sailed around the world on a tramp steamer, served in Special

Forces in Vietnam, done hard work or hard time, or lived in a New Orleans brothel. But it would be difficult for anyone to speak seriously of "the innocence of youth" or kindred ideas while staring into Doug's world-ravaged face: they had barely lived twenty years (Dan and Matt not even that) but they had done a great deal of living.

Not that drugs and drink and late nights by themselves make anybody especially hardcore, or if they do then most people over the age of fifteen are as much veterans of the psychic wars as Doug, Tom, Dan and Matt ever were. But the freaks' indisputable haggardness cannot be attributed only to long hours absorbing recreational chemicals, because there were other, grimmer, less material stresses shaping them. Family histories of divorce and alcoholism. Eating free meals at the local soup kitchen. Going home on an empty bus. Always using pay phones. Meeting old friends who had married, or converted to clean living. Hearing about old friends who had died. No money. No food. No time. Joe. There was the feeling that, however young they were chronologically, they were elderly in spirit, as they would while away the time going over their memories like old men, and they were as offended and confounded by modern culture and its high-tech slickness as any senior citizen. That intransigence became a point of pride for them. "A stick in the mud will hold its ground," Chris Bradshaw said.

This was not typical teenage pseudo-toughness, for the freaks never got nihilistic or narcissistically woe-is-us. They were not self-pitying but self-assured (at least as self-assured as they would ever be); it was their humanity and not their hormones that governed their actions and feelings. They were not going through any phases. Wisdom had come to them in hangovers and hitchhiking, in welfare cheques and walking along the train tracks, dotted with buttercups and clover and dandelions. It had been gained in bottle tokes and backstreets, in coffee shops at midnight, downtown and disheartened. They knew what it was like to be totally spent—their world-weariness was earned.

Pal died.

*

FROM THE BEGINNING, there were tensions between them. The clash of Doug's, Tom's, Dan's and Matt's personalities was such that they couldn't go very long without one of them getting pissed off at another, and on occasion the whole thing seemed pointless and futile, since they each were riddled with annoying traits that never failed to blister the nerves of the other three. It was an imperfect union.

Good ol' Dan was usually above reproach, as he was so bright and nice and good-natured, but he did have a couple of bad habits that got Doug, Tom and Matt rather peeved. He was notoriously unpunctual—he would blithely arrive anywhere from twenty minutes to several hours late for any appointment, and sometimes he never showed up at all, having been waylaid by an errand or an absorbing book or a previous engagement (and he was probably late for that one too). It got so bad that his estimated times of arrival had to be translated from "Dan time" to "real time," with "A little while, man" equalling ninety minutes and "Later tonight, all right?" meaning early the next morning. Dan was a terrible drinker, too: whatever amount of beverage he was allotted would wipe him out before his friends were even tipsy, and he would eagerly suck back more (or want to buy more), all the while saying

"I'm *ham*-mered." Then he would slip into a stupor, or pass out, and when he passed out it looked like he was in danger of passing away. Nothing could revive him. Once, when he was in Sudbury with his mother, he was found unconscious in a snowbank, full of lemon gin, and had to be rushed to the hospital with an acute case of alcohol poisoning. Another time he and Tom and Doug picked up three twenty-sixers of sherry at $4.50 a bottle (the money was meant for acid but they couldn't find any), and once again he ended up face down as his more controlled drinking buddies splashed water on him and dragged him around his backyard, eventually leaving him naked in bed before they stumbled homewards, exasperated (this came on the heels of his "I love you" incident with the JD). Amusing at the time, Tom and Doug both awoke the following morning to the sobering realization they had left a very drunk person out cold and alone. After trying Dan's number several times without response, Tom phoned Doug.

"There's no answer at Dan's," he said in a voice just above a whisper.

"I know, I've been calling too," Doug responded. Panic mounted. Tom rode the Black Plague through the train yards over to Lansdowne Avenue, imagining his trial and conviction for alcoholic manslaughter, and rang the bell once, twice, thrice, and again, until the pale remainder of Dan crept out to open the door, sick to death but blessedly, legally alive. In time, Matt and Tom lectured Dan so much that he took care not to get so incompetent —he still drank as heavily as he ever did, he just drank slower.

Matt himself had that talent for impenetrable headgames, and Doug and Tom in particular used to get frustrated with him because of it. He meant no harm, really—it was just that you had to decipher his wise-ass jibing and decide when he was being straightforward and when he was fucking you up. "You blow my mind, guy," Tom always said when he got befuddled. Then again, Matt could be simply short-tempered and rail into anyone who said or did anything dumb, and Dan was his usual victim. When he was first moving into the apartment by the Blue Boy, Dan had lost the keys to the place when (apropos of nothing) he tossed them up too high and they landed the freaks knew not where. Dan, typically, tried to put the best face on the situation, but Matt would have none of it.

"Well buddy, maybe you have an extra set of keys someplace…?"

"I have nothing—go home."

Or when Ray Deneault got thrown in the can for missing his court appearance, he was holding the only key to the place on Blucher he shared with Matt, leaving his roommate locked out. Matt had to retrieve the key, but the cop shop was a long ways away. Sitting around the Jive Hive, Dan, typically, was optimistic.

"Well buddy, why don't you take the bus up there?"

"With what, my fuckin' good looks?"

"Jesus, man, he was just making a suggestion," said Tom.

"He knows damn well I haven't got any money."

Condescension was Tom's main fault in the eyes of the others; though he tried to hide it he sometimes left them with the impression he would do things a lot differently if he was in their shoes. His periodic interludes of abstaining from booze and dope made him a little holier-than-thou, and his insufferably high principles on other matters could be irritating as well. There was in him more ant than grasshopper. Doug, one time, had grown tired of his friend's chiding over his drinking, and he turned to him and sighed, "A.A.?" Tom did have a tendency to try to reform people. He also used to get nasty whenever there was a debate going down: the four freaks loved to talk about politics and history and other weighty subjects, and it was always Tom who played angel's advocate, mulishly defending American foreign policy, or Brian Mulroney, or God, whenever he sensed disagreement. He would raise his voice and become sort of mean, like when he and Doug and Dan were coming home from a movie about cults and rituals called *The Believers*.

"Well," Dan began, "the whole idea of religion is basically—"

"Oh, fuck off, Dan."

Tom had to be quieted down now and again during discussions ("Take it easy, man, we're just rappin'"), and then he would sulk until he could lay another morality trip on everybody. Fucking guy.

The more he drank and the more he got stoned and the more hits he dropped, the more Doug appeared to be slipping into a hazardous area on the fringes of burnout. He was becoming moody and quarrelsome, and his regular energetic restlessness had turned into dissipated indifference. Despite his Jive Hive being the four freaks' most popular scene (or maybe that *was* the reason), he was increasingly aloof, and he was getting into trips without including Tom or Dan or Matt. If he wasn't hanging out with Deneault, he was with Michelle, his sometime girlfriend from Whitefish Falls, who came from university in Sudbury to spend a weekend with him now and again (she had been a flame of Dan's, in fact). As Doug kept going off on his own with whomever, and on whatever, the others started speaking in worried tones of "the three freaks."

There was one week in the spring that was an especially shitty one for them. Tom hadn't been around in a while—he was pouting back at his place, feeling left out and cut off from the excitement of the Blucher Boys. They were all localized and within easy reach of each other; he was stuck many blocks away, missing the everyday fuma fests and thinking, Well, fuck them if they just expect me to drop by.

Dan's conflict with Slime was getting violent. He and Joe had been sitting in his room when Richmond came in and gave them shit for something, and punctuated his reprimand by cuffing Dan on the head. A scuffle ensued, and a furious Dan stormed out of the house and went to stay with his brother, who was then living above an antique shop called The House of Treasures.

Michelle was visiting Doug at that point, and she had brought some magic mushrooms with her. Late one morning Matt came over to say hello—his normal routine—and chatted with the couple for a few minutes. But Doug's brain cells were still roasting by an open psilocybin fire, and his neighbour's industrial-strength sarcasm hit him at exactly the wrong moment. When he was back at his place Matt's doorbell rang, and he went downstairs to face a seething Doug who verbally tore into him, saying he'd had enough of Matt's bullshit, saying this and saying that, coming dangerously close to physical aggression. The confrontation had been a long time in coming, and it threatened to destroy everything. It was a very bad scene. Dan and Tom came to see Matt the next day, and the apartment was very quiet except for Deneault talking with his girlfriend and a Dylan tape bleakly playing "North Country Blues": "...*tell you now, the whole town is empty.*" Bad scene all around.

*

YET SOMEHOW they all held together, maybe because their bickerings and fallings-out were therapeutic—people as contrasting as the four freaks could only be expected to provoke each other every so often, and the erratic disposition of their friendship and the absence of corny clubbism might have been the very factors that sustained it. And inevitably, when they considered their unlikely sociality and the small scrap of extraordinariness it had brought to their mostly ordinary lives, they started to celebrate themselves as slightly more than a circle of chums. There was never anything "official" in this (no membership cards or badges or anything like that), but there was a laid-back esprit de corps among them, and an awareness of the peculiar family they comprised: Doug was the weird, wizened uncle, Tom was the shy, smartass nephew, Dan was the pesky kid brother and Matt was the grumpy-yet-lovable grandpa.

It was mainly softhearted Dan and Tom who went in for this group identity thing, against Doug's apathy and Matt's ridiculing of them as "saps," but it was hard to shake the sense of stoned fraternity that had been with them ever since the quartet had started gravitating together. "The four freaks" had such a pleasantly alliterative ring to it that it had to be their shared title; its silliness was exceeded only by its perfection, in the same way that the improbability of the group itself was exceeded only by its fragile harmony. That's where the music came in.

*

BESIDES BEING INTO good tunes, the four freaks could play tunes too—Doug had his flutes, Tom had his guitars and his harmonica, Dan had his guitar, his flute, and his recorder, and

Matt had sung with a band. It was natural that Dan, Tom and Doug would occasionally jam and trade techniques while partying, but it was more adventurous for all of them to write and record original songs. Though they never formed a real band with a bass and drums, and though they had no strong intention of making serious professional tapes, their music was no hobby. It was their self-expression, their art, and it gave them some of their best times.

When they were going to high school Doug and Tom had made cassettes full of their own stuff, with Doug singing liberally borrowed lyrics from Alice Cooper and Pink Floyd, and Tom tripping over primitive patterns on his feebly-amplified guitar. The duo called themselves Time, Distance & Speed, after Doug had read that smoking pot affected one's perceptions of those realities, and while they were not potential chart-toppers they had got a real kick from making their "albums" and hearing themselves improve with every effort. Doug had a full, raw voice, and he could write and improvise good lyrics, and his partner had a distinctive, if sloppy, style as a guitarist. They were still into making tapes by the time Dan and Matt arrived on their scene.

The other half of the four freaks had done some recording of their own. During their brief occupancy of the apartment on Huron Street they had made a ten-minute epic concisely entitled *Hell*, which was a sort of variety show set in the Inferno itself, hosted by Satan (played by Matt, who else?) and his assistant, Igor (played by Dan): "We have executions, torture, music, and other fun things lined up for today's program." Among the "fun things" was a delightful ditty about Bill Richmond, "a special example of what you have to do to come to Hell." Satan and Igor cited Slime for killing children ("Well, he usually buggers them before he kills them, I must add") and dwelling "in other people's crud," and they dubbed their ballad "Not Now, Bill, Take Your Dick Out of the Little Boy's Pants." Matt and Dan fucked around with more projects after Matt moved into the place near the Blue Boy, this time using an old organ for a tape called *Day of the Ass*, which was inspired by seeing an attractive female's on the street.

While Doug, Tom, Dan and Matt all dug the idea of laying tunes down for their own amusement (some people would have dismissed it as a waste of time), they'd been hanging out for some time before they began to collaborate musically. Originally they just left a ghetto blaster on "record" while they jammed and did free-form versions of Matt's and Dan's ode to Slime, but their first really promising sounds happened in the fall of 86, when Doug, Dan and Matt were on acid up at Lansdowne, a couple of days before Doug planned to leave to see Amy in Halifax. They were upstairs in the sun room, watching night come over the city and tripping heavily; Dan was strumming a little piece on his acoustic and Matt started to muse about the approaching farewells. "*What ever happened,*" he sang desolately, "*to Time, Distance and Speed? / They was cool in their time…*" Then he caught a wave of acid— "*This is gettin'…steadily depressin'…*" Dan's blaster captured the sad snatch of melody, and it became their first hit.

The big problem, though, was that they had no drums or decent percussion, making it hard to play anything truly rock 'n' roll. As Time, Distance & Speed Doug and Tom had banged cardboard boxes with knitting needles, and they had also used Joe's tambourine and bongos when he "produced" them with his four-track mixing board, but none of these were very adequate. It was when Matt got to borrow his girlfriend's brother's keyboard, with a drum machine built in, that the four freaks' music got the extra touch of professionalism it needed. Whereas drum machines made radio songs sound more synthetic and soulless than they already were, for amateurs they were economical and efficient, and the keyboard's multitude of tones added further to their arrangements.

And so cutting tunes got to be a regular freak activity. Much of their material was no doubt of the You-had-to-be-there variety, because they never troubled to really polish any of their stuff, and the majority of it was made up after any number of BTs had been knocked back. They knew enough to play on tempo and in the same key, but that was about the extent of their musicianship. The sound quality was always lo-fi, a result of recording through the condenser microphones of portable stereos, but this didn't deter them—over dozens of sessions they came up with some pretty cool cuts. There was "Frustration in a Nutshell," a muddy, scorching number they pounded out with Dan and Tom on acoustic and electric guitars respectively, Matt handling the keyboard and playing drum fills, and Doug making up wicked lyrics as he went along; they did a ragged but sizzling cover of "All Along the Watchtower," and "Gotta Get Away" had Tom taking a turn on vocals. "People Come, People Go" was a solid slab of hard rock that showcased the freaky interplay of Tom and Dan on six-strings, with Dan chugging out his strummy, swinging chords and Tom discarding his usual mellow licks to do some screaming lead. And Matt had several way-out works where he experimented with the keyboard and uttered scarifying demonic nonsense into the blaster.

On a single memorable evening they laid down four quality tracks while getting high around the table in the Jive Hive. They began with what was later rightly named "Loose End," a vague but upbeat coalescence of guitars, drums, and flute, and next they did a grungy blues piece Tom had written called "I Take My New Woman," tailor-made for Doug's wracked pipes. Moving along productively, they did "Doom of the Damned" (alternate title "Coming Back to Earth"), which ominously combined Dan's descending chord progression, Tom's distorted barre chords, Doug's flute and Matt's wispy keyboard; this segued into "In Search of the Fourth Dimension," wherein Matt took over and challenged the others to keep up with his evilly quickening rhythms, and Doug blurted creepy inaudible words—something about weaving no morals and weaving no shame. "Satanic Jingle Bells," Tom termed it. That was a really good scene, that whole night, and it was preserved on a cassette: *The Four Freaks Live in the Jive Hive*.

Among all their informal snippets that came together almost accidentally (one tape opened with a thunk and Dan slurring, "...I thought we'd *been* recording"), two completed compositions stand out. "Jagged Edge" was a tight, grinding song that Matt and Dan had conceived, and it got recorded with Tom contributing a guitar solo and Joe colouring it with some echo, through his fourtrack. The session took place on a sunny afternoon in the attic of Matt's on Blucher, which had started to resemble Abbey Road studios, cluttered with electric and acoustic guitars, amplifiers, microphones, the keyboard, cords, and tape players. After doing some BTs and recovering from the initial head rush, the musicians ran through the basic structure of the tune, and then got it down in a couple of takes. The solo was right on, and the echo helped too, but it was basically a Tremblay-Wright creation: it strongly featured Dan playing a huge, electrified rhythm that was still "power pop" in the tradition of Beatle classics like "Ticket to Ride" and "Nowhere Man," and Matt sang with a belting, achingly defeated voice. "*I wake at the noon hour / The day blooms in gold*," went one line ("See," he explained, "that's about gettin' up at noon and blowin' a big reef"), and the bridge was poignant: "*I don't wanna go there / I've been there before / And if I hit that jagged edge / I'll say goodbye no more.*" It ended with the freaks applauding their performance and Matt asking "Who are those guys?" like a drunk cheering some potent bar band. Musically "Jagged Edge" was a great cross of hard rock and hummable melody, and lyrically it was a masterpiece of heartbreak.

But "Storm Song" was their all-time anthem. This originated with Tom, who thought up a simple passage of A-B minor-D minor to be repeated throughout the number, although he couldn't write any verses that didn't sound heavy-handed. He and Dan worked on it for a while, and developed it along their patented twin-guitar style, with Dan strumming with drive and finesse and Tom picking soulful little phrases over top. They then brought it to Doug, who was brooding in the Jive Hive, and he seemed noncommittal, as he was about most things at the time, but they figured they'd do it that night anyway. Matt brought his keyboard over, and a dude by the name of Bruce Kerr, who'd played bass in Lone Faith, came in with his twelve-string. Deneault was there as well, looking for more dope, so he was included in the ensemble, given maracas. The six of them tuned up and practiced, practiced and tuned up again, and all the time Doug was scrawling verses on a scrap of paper, for Tom had left him to give the song voice. Usually Doug sang other-worldly lyrics about dragons and pixies and the Tarot, but just before they were to record Dan and Tom read what he had jotted down and were struck by his candour and his heartfelt mourning.

They did one take that wasn't very good (the phone had rung halfway through—it was Rick), but they were encouraged to try another. One more tuning-up, and then Doug simultaneously pressed "Play" and "Record" on his blaster, and Dan, anchoring the group as rhythm guitarist, said "All right." He fingerpicked the intro tenderly, as Matt accompanied him with delicate measures from the keyboard, and Doug joined in with a melancholy flute. After a few bars of this Dan started strumming his guitar, and the rest of the band kicked in: Tom did his licks, Bruce Kerr gave weight to Dan's rhythm, and Deneault shook the maracas dubiously but in time. And then Doug began to sing.

It seems to me things have fallen
Below what they used to be
And it seems for us the storm is comin'
Drown what we are and used to be...
No turnin' back, no exit, no return
No bleedin' heart my soul to burn
Pulled under now in the river's waves
Strong as fire 'til the rain comes...
It seems to me the world's crumblin' quick
Ain't no saviour today
And it seems for us the fire's burnin' quick
There ain't no way to pay...
It seems for us the end's a day away...
Storm song
Not too long...

It flowed on for a long time, with Doug wailing away as the others drove forward, airy and forceful. Tom, Dan and Matt played knowing that Doug was singing what he would never say, that he was lamenting the friendship that had been clouded over, lessened, the friendship with an end that was a day away. All the neglect, all the coldness, and all the hurt feelings between them were washed away in the rains of "Storm Song," because in its grieving was the acknowledgment that there was something to grieve; the torrent of emotion revealed a deep concern that was not only moving but consoling. When it ended in a short flurry of notes from Dan, there was a stunned, changed silence in the Jive Hive, and Tom just said "Fuckin' right," which said it all. It was the four freaks' finest song, and perhaps the four freaks' finest moment.

*

THAT THE FREAKS' best music was wistful and bittersweet wasn't coincidental, for the sentiments expressed in "Jagged Edge," "Storm Song," and the rest were the same ones that pervaded their whole lives. A feeling of restrained sorrow, of casual dejection, was always with them—there were more endings than beginnings in their world, and everything they said or did was tinged with abandon and desperation. They were used to things constantly fucking up: relatively minor pissoffs like Tom's Black Plague falling apart, for example, but also the subtle tragedies of Dan fighting with Slime and his mom, or Doug's and Matt's precarious domestic circumstances, which were jostled from welfare lines to soup kitchens to landlords to grocery stores to drug connections. Even otherwise happy scenes, like a good jam or a good party, seemed to be but temporary levelings-off in the overall decline of their existence.

Because loss was felt everywhere, it wasn't felt at all. They would register dissatisfaction or frustration with every heaping of bullshit, but they were too numbed to let any of it get to them. They found fragments of joy where they could, and joy was valuable, but it was contentment that was the really elusive prize, and they had almost given up the search for that. There was nothing much they could do to improve their lots, so what the fuck, get stoned and get drunk, play tunes and hang out, nothing else going down. If sitting around and rapping of old times and dead friends offered a short respite from their troubles, why not? They daydreamed out loud to each other, imagining scenarios of vintage guitar collections, massive stereos, and fruit jars filled with oil; they thought longingly of their futures while dreading the next day. Joe had a song called "Someday When I'm Famous," about their wishfulness, their belief that although times were bad and getting worse, there was still a possibility of something good down the road. Despair was warded off again and again and again.

*

THE JIVE HIVE's days were numbered. Larocque was moving out to live with his girlfriend, and once more Doug was left with the rent, which he just couldn't pay by himself. He asked his friends if any of them wanted to share the place with him, and both Rick and Dan said maybe, but in the end they had to back out. Doug would have to leave.

There were still a couple of weeks before he needed to vacate, though, and the four freaks made sure they took the opportunity to live out the term of the Blucher Boys with fun and frequent parties. Matt and Doug had affected a cagey reconciliation that had Dan and Tom acting as buffers between them, and the group seemed to have returned to its unsteady unity. As the days were growing longer, they would often stroll down to the river where they had found a lovely lookout spot that was on the other side of a little foot bridge. Here they spent dusks seeing the moon rise and watching the huge cargo ships of the Great Lakes pass through the locks. It was a contemplative scene, not made for Frisbees or loud fucking around—they would just lean against the guardrail and ponder the water and the sky and the cityscape; they might smoke a joint or two, and listen to Tom blow his harmonica, and they would talk and think and then amble back to Blucher as night began to fall.

Doug had found another apartment to take, but as he wasn't sure when Larocque was going to get his shit out of the Jive Hive he had no set date for moving himself. This new pad was fairly close by, actually—it was on the second floor of the back of Alex's Lunch, a restaurant on Bruce Street that was but a few minutes' walk from Blucher or Lansdowne—but it was terribly small, having only one room and a can, and neither a fridge nor a stove, and was fitted with large windows that promised to turn it into an oven on hot afternoons. It was a real letdown from the accommodations he was used to, but it was all Doug could afford on his income from Futures.

Early one grey evening towards the end of May the freaks were lazing about the Jive Hive for what would turn out to be the last time. Matt had gone back to his place to crash, complaining of a headache, but Doug, Tom and Dan were still there when Larocque unexpectedly pulled up in a big van that he'd borrowed from Budget. He had decided that the move would be done that night, and since the apartment at Alex's Lunch was already empty,

Doug, though caught off guard, guessed it would be all right to go ahead with things. So the ex-roommates and Dan and Tom hauled boxes of books and clothes and dishes, and mattresses and chairs and posters and all the bits and pieces that had made up the site of good times, bad times out into the hold of the van. Up and down the stairs, up and down, up and down, carrying away chunks of a world until, within half an hour, there was nothing left but reverberations in empty rooms. Clay was there with his kids, standing around, seeing that everything went okay and bidding the guys an easygoing goodbye.

When they had done all the loading Larocque drove Doug and Dan and Tom over to the new place, where Doug's belongings (including a portable cage occupied by Yang the cat) were lugged up a shaky outdoor wooden staircase, and left in the cubicle that was to be his home. Deneault showed up, and so did a friend of Larocque's named Corey, who wanted to score some dope. The six of them milled around the parking lot and the back laneway—Doug's "yard," now—and they noticed a bookcase that the apartment's previous tenants, a bunch of punkers, had thrown out. It was covered in the usual shock-value punk graffiti: "FUCK OFF RONNIE," "EAT SHIT AND DIE," and so forth. "Did you see this?" Tom asked Doug.

"Yeah," was the inattentive reply. "Pretty gutless."

Then it was off to Larocque and his girlfriend's in the west end, which was in a building surrounded by a proverbial white picket fence, and inside it was equally suburban, with shag carpeting and a waterbed and all the accessories necessary for a nice young modern couple. More stuff was brought up more stairs, and then after their exertions they had some beer and burned some of the oil Corey had picked up. Doug looked at the living room's main piece of art, a poster of a kitten eyeing a goldfish in a bowl. "What are you doin' in that bowl, Danny?" he asked his old friend, and Larocque glowered back at him. The van had to be returned, so Doug, Larocque, Tom and Dan and Deneault piled in and headed back. It had been raining while they were lifting things into the pad, but it wasn't anymore.

In the bare back of the van were Dan and Tom and Deneault, who said it reminded him of being in a paddy wagon, all dark, and Dan and Tom were very stoned, sitting down facing rearwards. Dan was pretending he was on a train, Tom said fuck that, he was on the fuckin' starship Enterprise, and they screamed gleefully every time they went around a corner, and up front Larocque was telling them to shut up because cops were driving alongside and they might hear. And there was Doug in the passenger's seat, smiling sadly, not saying anything, thinking about the cell-like place he would be living in, thinking about his Jive Hive and wondering how his life could be packed away into ever fewer cardboard boxes.

The "Anti-Room," as the pad at Alex's Lunch was half-heartedly referred to, never took on the accessibility of the Jive Hive, for in size and location it definitely left a lot to be desired. They did party there a few times, and Doug welcomed the chance to have guests, but it was Matt's apartment that the freaks congregated at more commonly. From the time he had moved there its spaciousness had made it popular with him and his friends, and now it became the usual scene of fuma fests and jams. They still went to their hangout on the river, and Dan's backyard was once more attractive on sunny days when his mom and Slime weren't around. Even Rick, who lived down closer to Tom's house, started to receive visitors, notwithstanding his inclination to subject them to wrestling videos and Willie Nelson tapes. Some kind of transformation was going on in those days; there was change in the air but no one knew how it would next materialize.

*

IT WAS THE beginning of the summer of 1987—Doug, Tom, Dan and Matt had been getting together for one year. Those original joints that had been passed around in Dan's kitchen were long gone, but the results of their being passed had defiantly endured. The four freaks were still around.

Lakeway closed. Matt and Dan, and Rick too, watched the flag-lowering ceremony and admitted to being sorry to see the school die, which was sort of lost on Doug and Tom, who were free of their old alma mater and didn't miss it at all. Dan celebrated Lakeway's last day of classes by showing up piss-drunk, lurching around the hallways until a teacher told him to get out, and at an alumni reunion he again got tanked. All the freaks were hitting the sauce at the time, for the weather was hot and drinking was more refreshing than throat-searing bottle tokes. Acid was around a lot as well, and with the exception of Tom, who had still not dropped, everyone was catching rides on the LSD train. Doug and Dan and Rick got into some particularly high-powered hits one night and tripped down to the water, and Doug had what might have been an out-of-body experience. The following day he was still quaking through a chemical hangover and he had to wear shades to prevent sensory overload, and as he was sitting obliterated in the soup kitchen, having a coffee, a big Indian sat down by him and said what he least needed to hear:

"Y'know, you look like the guy who ripped me off for an oh-zee [ounce of weed, worth a dangerous amount of cash] a ways back."

Incredibly, Doug didn't lose control—he just removed his sunglasses and let the accuser see the piss-holes in the snow where his eyes once were, and uttered, "Hey man, I don't know nothin' about your dope." The case of mistaken identity ended right there.

There was one more recording session that they all took part in, producing a tune called "The End (Do It All Over Again)." It was a follow-up to "Storm Song" that didn't quite have the sonic punch of the earlier tune, but its lyrics, which they each took turns writing and vocalizing, signalled that they had at last recognized their value to each other as friends.

Dan sang first:

> *A long time ago I thought I knew*
> *All the perfect answers to*
> *All the questions in my mind's eye*
> *Sitting in the corner of a room*
> *Knowing the end is coming soon*
> *And all I can do is sit and wonder why*

Then Matt:

> *Time it has gone and passed me by*
> *I think not of where or why*
> *All I do is hope and try again*
> *Waiting for the morning light*
> *I can see no end in sight*
> *All that's left to do is say my lines*

Tom:

> *I'm livin' on my own*

> *I guess I've always been*
> *But I've seen a lot of faces passin' through*
> *I'm in my little zone*
> *Do you know what I mean?*
> *But I won't be strayin' far from you*

And Doug:

> *I come again to this ancient place*
> *There are no tears upon my face*
> *When you scream you won't be heard*
> *Above the roar of the sea*
> *Above the roar of the city*

Matt and Doug harmonized on the stream-of-consciousness chorus:

> *Do it all over again*
> *Lost in this tangled web*
> *Diving through the wire*
> *Screaming in this choir*
> *'cause my thoughts are burning higher*
> *Every dog it shall expire*

*

BUT IT WAS ironic that only with these lines could they confess themselves, because it was all too late to matter. Doug was kicked out of Futures for telling someone to shut her mouth, and for general insubordination, so he had no money and was going to leave the Sault. And Tom had been saying he wanted to get out for a while, and it appeared he was going to seize the opportunity his older sisters had presented, whereby he would stay with them in Toronto while he tried to break into the movie business. The four freaks were splitting up.

Doug was heading out first. He cleared out the Anti-Room, after living in it barely a month, and he abandoned most of his things to his parents and to the other freaks. Rick had formulated a strategy with him: Doug would live in Whitefish Falls with Michelle for a month or two during the summer, and then he would join Rick in Windsor, where Rick would be securing a couple of jobs in a factory where his brother worked. Everyone knew there was more work down south. That was where you had to go. By 1987 the city's sinking economy had made popular a bitter local wisecrack: "Will the last person to leave the Sault please turn out the lights?"

They held a farewell party at the apartment Rick had shared with his mother (she'd left town herself), and it was a farewell not just to Doug but to their wholeness. It was a farewell to everyone. They downed vodka and peach schnapps, and smoked big joints stuffed with weed, and Tom smoked himself into temporary immobility, wondering if he would spend the rest of his life in the chair where he sat. Doug briefly disappeared and came back with Yang, the feline freak, who Matt would inherit. They went up to the roof garden (there wasn't any garden, just a patio of gravel) and looked down on Queen Street and the few remaining stragglers of nightlife still searching for a bar, or for home, and they were rapping and buzzing out. Dan found Rick's camera and ran off to buy some film, returning with just enough for twelve pictures, which they took of each other in varying stages of wastedness. There were two exposures left when Tom and Dan asked Rick to get a couple of the four freaks together, just to preserve the memory, and they all came to sit next to each other on the edge of the roof, an epitaph that was their final convergence, their final act of oneness. Rick froze them with a flash, capturing the moment they once and for all conceded the affection that was between them: Matt muttered about "saps," Dan smiled, Tom smirked and Doug tried to look alive. After that they stuporously went back inside for the bash's epilogue. Doug would spend the night there before going to Whitefish Falls, and Dan was going with him for a few days—there was a folk festival in Sudbury he wanted to see. In the early hours they shook hands and staggered off. It was yet another ending, another closing chapter, another world crumblin' quick.

*

A COUPLE OF WEEKS later, in early July, Tom fucked off to TO. There was a goodbye get-together for him too, where he and Dan and Matt finished off a forty of vodka and a lot of grass, beginning up at Lansdowne in the afternoon, continuing in the wooded gully behind St. Mary's College, and winding up at Matt's at about five in the morning. They were drunk and stoned, but they were able to cut a tune, "Black-Eyed Susan," in the merciful dimness of Matt's living room. "*It's all right girl, don't be blue,*" Matt rasped over the drum machine, Tom's thumping bass notes, and the gentle weeping of Dan's acoustic, "*I'm not goin' 'cause of you / There's many things I got to do / It's all right girl, don't be blue.*" From the despondency of the verses the chorus emerged triumphant:

> *Oooh, Black-Eyed Susan*
> *Oooh, don't you cry*
> *Oooh, Black-Eyed Susan*
> *This ain't the last goodbye*

The tape caught Rick and Matt's brother Mark Wright talking in the background (Deneault was gone at that point—he had vanished suddenly and the next anyone heard he was in jail in Kingston), but that only gave it a folky realism. When the session was over they listened to their song a bunch of times, and Dan was saying "The four freaks will never die," which drew laughter even from sentimental Tom, but they kept replaying "Black-Eyed Susan" into the break of dawn. *This ain't the last goodbye.* A day later, Dan waved to Tom in the Howes' car as it drove by him on its way to the airport.

*

"THE FOUR FREAKS were never seen again together," Matt spoke forbiddingly into his blaster's microphone as he picked out doom-laden chords on the keyboard. "Douglas Davis became the leader of a Satanic cult somewhere around Windsor, Ontario. Thomas Howe became a famous movie director and producer and was known among the likes of Kubrick and Coppola. Daniel R. Tremblay became a seclusive author and now writes novels somewhere in northern Canada. As for me—" Here the sounds change and Matt just laughs in that wicked way of his.

But contrary to such terminal where-are-they-nows, the four freaks were seen again together, for dramatic, decisive conclusions had never been one of their strong points. They stayed in touch and continued to make contact in spite of the distances between them. Nobody really expected it all to just end. But that single year in Sault Ste. Marie did end; that never came back. It had receded into the territory of remembrance. It was gone for good.

The essence of the freaks, all of them in their circle, was a curious mixture of small-town street smarts and cultivated intelligence, in that they smoked dope and rocked on to Led Zeppelin one minute and then played chess and recited Coleridge the next.

Their lives had room enough for Harley Davidsons and Harlan Ellison, for soup kitchens and Scott Fitzgerald, for hash oil and oil paintings, for electric guitars and wooden flutes. It was a duality that made them an invisible quasi-underground, too natural to be stylish bohemians, too bright to be crude rednecks, too philosophical to be disaffected activists. They were agreeably alienated. They were offhand outcasts. Their temporal and geographical setting of northern Ontario in the 1980s made them feel doubly isolated, both by the kind of rugged, worn-down city they lived in, and by the time's pastel-glitzy culture of *Miami Vice* on TV and Cyndi Lauper on the radio. When they got together to smoke and play older, better music, it really seemed to them as if they were some fugitive sect, hiding from the Just Say No police, Pat Robertson on *The 700 Club*, and the Top 40 charts. "*Heatscore!*" someone would warn whenever they risked exposure. "Not here—*heatscore!*" People have always been getting stoned in private groups, but there was something about that era and that situation that made them all feel like they were gathering at little oases of freedom and fun in a great desert of arid straightness and repression. Maybe it was just being nineteen and needing somewhere to go.

The essence of the four freaks is something different. Whatever they made together in the months from the summer of 1986 to the summer of 1987, and however they prevented it from falling apart, it amounted to no more than the spontaneous, fleeting friendship of young men, sometimes strained and grudging at that. As four separate, distinct individuals, all Doug, Tom, Dan and Matt ever did was to form a bond where there was none before—but if they could do no better than that, they still did as well as anyone ever does. None of this is unique, or important, but it is all true.

Part III

The West Wind

Victim of Changes

THE FOLK SINGER Phil Ochs had a song called "There But For Fortune" in which he recast archetypal down-and-outers—a convict, a hobo, a drunkard—as, after all, formerly young men who had full lives and limitless opportunities stretching before them. I thought of this after I spent a day visiting an old friend I'll call Joe, in a city a morning's trip away from my own. I'd first met Joe twenty-five years before, in Grade Six, and we and a handful of other boys had grown up together; Joe was always the most unconventional of us, but over the years he had gone further and further down the tunnel of indulgence and incaution, had suffered a disastrous too-young marriage and the too-young death of his devoted mother, and I found him and his surroundings to be about as seedy as his history had led me to expect. Before introducing him to my girlfriend some time previously, I'd described him as a poet, freelance recording engineer and pirate radio broadcaster, but a few days' stay at our place left a different impression: Joe had a heart of gold, she said, but he was going nowhere fast. "*There, but for fortune…*" If this was an innocence-to-experience drama I would be the sensitive one who became a writer, and Joe would be the daredevil who gambled with fate a few too many times and became the lost soul.

Joe was living in a house with an assortment of odd characters, including his girlfriend Linda, some years his senior, and her teenage daughter. They were all addicted to cigarettes, alcohol, and marijuana. No one seemed to be working; Joe played guitar and busked occasionally, agonizing through Bob Dylan's "One More Cup of Coffee" and John Lennon's "Working Class Hero" for loose change. He was getting a disability cheque once a month for, I guess, being who he was. A younger brother, also a pal of mine from way back, was experiencing an emotional crisis on the other side of the country, and Joe was fraught with the project of rescuing him away. An older guy, Harry, was crashing there and earning his keep by bringing in items like jewellery and stereo equipment, which he claimed to find in dumpsters and junk heaps. He had done odd jobs around Canada, including in Red Lake, Ontario, before hooking up with Joe ("I paid bills and all that for six years, after my wife died," Harry told me, which was explanation enough). A sense of barely concealed petty criminality hovered just out of sight. Joe's whole scene seemed at the limits of "sordid," looking over the border at "squalor." I played guitar, drank beer, and smoked dope with him, for old times' sake, and caught the last ferry home that evening, staring out at the water.

As a public problem, conservatives would write Joe off as a drain on society, while liberals would cite Joe as a casualty of it. As a friend, I remembered that he and I had once shared appetites for drink and drugs and rock 'n' roll, and then two decades went by and somehow much of that commonality had gone. Now Joe and his circle wandered in a private haze of poverty and decadence, waste and thrift, self-destruction and self-pity. With so little of anything to his name, he cultivated a high sensitivity to having his name impugned, and with endless time to kill he had become terribly high-strung: he was no longer a really nice, laid-back guy. Still basically decent underneath but badly coarsened on the outside, his character had become a jackal's. He was, I saw, just a damaged human being, and whether the damage had been done by himself or the rest of the world didn't matter.

It wasn't so much that he couldn't hold a job if he wanted to, but that he couldn't even want to hold a job. An adolescence and adulthood of consciously or unconsciously emulating Jack Kerouac and Keith Richards had corroded his capacity to organize his affairs, meet his commitments and monitor his health—irresponsibility was a perverse point of pride with him. Perhaps in the same way that some desperate citizen of the Third World might see conscription into a suicidal jihad as a step up in life, so did Joe see the regimen of welfare days, liquor stores, drug connections and pawn shops to be a welcome imposition of order on his chaotic reality. To me it was pointless and sad, but I knew Joe was doing pretty much what he wanted to do, what he had been doing for years, and doing it as well and as deliberately as ever, certainly better than I could have in the same circumstances. Feeling sorry for him would have been redundant. He was content in his frustrations.

How did we come to be so different? I too had absorbed the

philosophies of Beat freedom and rock star recklessness, and at seventeen or eighteen I considered Joe a hometown compatriot and creative collaborator. But I'd finished high school and he hadn't, learned to adapt to the constraints of landlords and employers while he chafed under any obligation, and stayed just sober and straight enough to play the Game when he was determined to keep partying hard, fuck the System. Joe had been Joe all along, I realized, and it was me who had become someone else. It had taken many years for me not to disdain as phony or frivolous anyone who was not there with me inhaling BTs in a hideaway in Sault Ste. Marie between 1984 and 1987—often I would find myself secretly measuring strangers or relatives or coworkers against the people I partied with in those places, deciding they had never reached the *in extremis* levels of wit and insight and feeling we had found together in the Jive Hive. My standards gradually slipped, but Joe's had not.

He had been given a reputation as the freakiest freak of them all, to whom the rules could never apply, and like a typecast actor he came to inhabit his role all too completely. In 1984, though, being Joe was a more positive and more promising adventure than the shabby, scavenging enterprise it turned out to be in the new millennium. Then, we tried to approximate Haight-Ashbury for ourselves, all sunshine and back laneways, all strummed acoustics and bags of weed, with "Desiderata" posted on his bedroom wall; now, Joe was still trying, but the effort had taken a grim toll. What was once bright idealism had become a day-to-day instinct for survival. It wasn't entirely his fault—I thought of his late mother, like his roommate Harry's late wife—and I could not suppress a guilty sense that I had been among those who had prodded him into the identity in which he was now confined. But I still missed my old friend, I was still hurt to see this troubled, troubling counterfeit, and I still counted myself lucky that I had not taken the same paths as he, that I had not done what he had done and seen what he had seen.

Sad Wings of Destiny

Tears, idle tears, I know not what they mean,
Tears from the depth of some divine despair
Rise in the heart and gather to the eyes,
In looking on the happy Autumn fields,
And thinking of the days that are no more.

Fresh as the first beam glittering on a sail,
That brings our friends up from the underworld,
Sad as the last which reddens over one
That sinks with all we love below the verge;
So sad, so fresh, the days that are no more.
—Tennyson, from "The Princess"

I FIRST MET DAN TREMBLAY when he was no more than six or seven and his older brother, with whom I shared an elementary school class, introduced him to me with some pride. Dan was doing well in grade one, explained Joe (he and I were about five years older, which was then a significant gap), and had just placed highly in a spelling bee. He was a fair-haired kid who smiled hopefully, and I wished him the best. Some things never change.

Years later I was still hanging out with Joe Tremblay, although we'd gone on to different high schools and I was still on the way to completing my education whereas he'd kind of lost interest after grade eleven. Dan was still around too, and now our age difference didn't seem so wide; Joe and I were into playing guitar, smoking dope and drinking (he used to get cheap red wine that was labelled with a stark military-style stencil—"RED WINE"), and listening to the Beatles and Bob Dylan, and Dan was generously included in our parties. I remember he could drink an entire bottle of beer in five seconds. He was then fourteen or so.

Gradually, between 1984 and 1986, Dan became a friend of mine in his own right. There was a loose network of us, including Dan and Joe and myself, schoolmates and former schoolmates, acquaintances and friends of friends, who had in common a taste for getting high and getting drunk, plus an appreciation for out-of-date rock music from the 60s and 70s and a casual contempt for the predicament of being young men growing up in a struggling northern Ontario steel town during the era of Brian Mulroney, Boy George, and *Top Gun*. It all was, and is, a pretty routine story of male bonding and coming of age, but the twist is in how we could see that all along, and how we were all curious to see how it would all play out and which roles we would enact.

> He simply wasn't interested in the day-to-day business of prosaic things. His heart and his mind

were free and untrammelled and, in his own way, perhaps, he was smarter than his elders; none of whom could say they actually disliked him and none of whom could admit, even to themselves, that they got half as much fun out of just being alive.
—F/L D.A. MacMillan, R.C.A.F.,
Only the Stars Know

Back then Dan Tremblay was a very charming teenage boy: good-looking, naturally sociable, obviously intelligent. He was attractive to girls and polite to their parents; he held civilized conversations with his teachers and sang and played guitar and flute with his buddies; he was a family peacemaker between Joe, his mother, and the middle brother Peter; and he was a well-known and well-liked student at Lakeway Collegiate. As I got to know him I found he was hugely idealistic and upbeat, always hospitable when I went to see him (he shared a bag of donuts with me saying, "Dig deeply, my friend"), and, rare in a young guy, willing to confess to a deep sentimentality over emotional episodes, or memories, or music—*I shed a tear at that moment*, he would admit. He bore little ill will to anyone and assumed he had none coming. My own parents were always happy to see him or have him call for me. "Hello, there," he would pipe over the phone, and I'd be summoned to speak to "your cheerful friend, Dan." I always picture that era in our lives as an early summer's towering blue sky, arched high above the city's rocks and trees and river, daubed with distant billowy clouds by day and sprinkled with stars as evening came down.

There were only a few dark spots on Dan's horizon, and none of us took much notice. Though a sturdy stoner and careful taker of LSD, he was not a good drunk—there were many occasions when Dan was so copious and enthusiastic a drinker he blacked out or passed out while everyone else stayed just moderately loaded, and when we all jammed together more than four or five beer badly cut into his guitar chops. Our friend Matt commented on how, on especially late and liquefied nights, the only thing holding Dan upright was his acoustic six-string and his steady repetition of his beloved D and G chords. Of our little pickup band, we kidded each other that Dan was its Brian Jones, the founder of the Rolling Stones who was ejected for chronic intoxication in 1969 and who drowned in his swimming pool shortly thereafter. Dan loved many things, and being really wrecked was high on the list.

And while there wasn't much he disliked, what he did he loathed. Dan had a slim but intense streak of hostility in him, usually vented harmlessly at "pigdogs," "arrogant yuppie scum," and other abstract bogeys of the conservative establishment, but sometimes aimed squarely at real individuals like his mom's on-again, off-again boyfriend (Dan called him only "Slime") or any unsympathetic educators or administrators he came up against. Smarter than most others his age and aware of it, he coasted through many of his courses and prided himself on coming through at the last minute to get the passing mark or meet the crucial deadline: he enjoyed telling of how, stoned to the point of oblivion in class, he had answered a suspicious teacher's question with a lucid and succinct summary that rounded off the entire lesson. Very competent and very confident, Dan had few reasons to worry. He was very young—so were we all.

Other, bigger, locales lured us away, singly and in pairs. Dan was not the first to leave, being a few years our junior and still finishing high school. It was then that I began to hear reports, and see firsthand, that Dan's organizational abilities were falling in inverse proportion to his drinking. He'd had a girlfriend or two, and he was good enough to come down to see me in Toronto for a weekend (I think he'd tried to pawn his flute for the bus fare), but there were early signs that his tendencies for lateness and half-completion were becoming entrenched. Once I was home for Christmas and he called me to ask if I had kept any of my old English or History papers that he could hand in for his own assignments (I hadn't). Already he was taking on the traits of the con man, forever talking his way out of trouble and positive he could turn on the charm to cruise to an easy success without having to strain himself too much. There were also tales of burned clothes, smashed windows, and minor injuries, as Dan navigated frequent drunken adventures on his none-too-trusty "autopilot." The sky was a little more full of clouds now.

> We were not ordinary. We were three tipsy young gods, incredibly wise, gloriously genial, and without limit to our powers. Ah!—and I say it now, after the years—could John Barleycorn keep one at such a height, I should never draw a sober breath again. But this is not a world of free freights. One pays according to an iron schedule—for every strength the balanced weakness; for every high a corresponding low; for every fictitious god-like moment an equivalent time in reptilian slime. For every feat of telescoping long days and weeks into mad, magnificent instants, one

> must pay with shortened life, and, oft-times, with savage usury added.
>
> —Jack London, *John Barleycorn*

But then many of us partied too hard and had psychological hang-ups, so it would have been hypocritical to single out Dan for his failings without conceding our own. For a year and a few months, in fact, Dan was my roommate in Ottawa, and there were some great times. He and I had both made it to university—he ahead of me, actually—and we briefly lived the undergrad life together. His long-range ambition had become environmental law, an arena where he could war with the big corporations and take the pigdogs to task. Before he dropped or transferred credits we shared exactly one lecture in a history class, where I recall him pointing out correctly that "communism" could still be found in Canada, in the form of back-to-the-land co-operative farms: he and our comrade Doug had once attempted to hitch-hike from our hometown to a commune called The Dandelion Project, so he knew whereof he spoke. Dan was juggling two girlfriends at this point, tearing off to Kingston or Guelph to see each of them, unbeknownst to the other. He had a Brian Mulroney mask and I had a sixteen-millimetre movie camera, which we took up to Parliament Hill to take footage of the PM staggering around inebriated. And one night his brother Peter, now working as a computer programmer, stayed over with us and I played guitar while he and Dan harmonized on the Stones' "Sweet Black Angel." There were some lovely moments in our little apartment.

Dan continued to drink a lot, however, and I found myself complaining to other people that he was just not a very responsible guy. Rent days might find him out of town, with one of the girlfriends, and once I came home to find him passed out (or gone out, I can't recollect) with an element on the stove left on red hot. Some of our gang, like Matt or Rick or Glen, had by now decided Dan was an accident-prone, incorrigible boozer—still a buddy and still full of fun, but nobody you'd trust to meet any kind of commitment. For two summers Dan earned money at the arduous job of tree planting in the north, and I respected his stamina, but then he'd return to Ottawa and revert to his spendthrift, scrounging style. There were calls to our place from banks and student loan officers; he was starting to dodge debts and final notices, increasingly falling back on his smooth-talk tactics and yet quite certain he could pull everything together when and how he chose.

Or was he? Dan knew and admitted his decision-making skills were weak, and with a wide range of options before him (not getting any wider, though), he was seized with introspection. As much as he would pledge tidy resolutions and guaranteed accomplishments in his future, there seemed to be a semi-conscious will to fail lurking deep inside him. He and I had a long quiet discussion in our living room one night as he considered whether he should stay in Ottawa for a summer term, or find a local job, or plant trees again, or return home, or go to Angela in Kingston. He picked over every choice, defending his judgement as sound and sensible one minute and then throwing up his hands the next—it was, by then, classic Dan, a contrary whirl of hubris and regret, hesitation and bravado. Finally I said, "Man, you're fucked." "Yeah, I know," he agreed. I saw him off at the bus terminal that midnight, bound back for the steel town whence we had come. It was springtime, 1992.

That summer, I heard the news that Dan's mother had died. She'd suffered from asthma and was out in the bush when she'd had an attack; she was alone and without medication; I don't think she was even fifty years old. I did up a homemade sympathy card, showing a picture of the sunny, secluded back garden she loved and where her sons and their friends had lazed about with guitars and beer and hash oil. "She was a good woman," I wrote to Joe, Peter, and Dan, "and I hope you guys will be all right without her." For several years I only heard of or from Dan intermittently, as I moved in with my girlfriend and later settled out in Vancouver. I was busy and so was he.

When I saw him again, in British Columbia, he was in his mid-twenties and had hardened without really maturing. He was full of stories of his mother's death, the resultant loss of her home which had been his base, his breakup with Angela, bad scrapes with pissed-off Indians and gay men, and his truncated trip to Europe which saw him go several days without food, stranded in Gibraltar. He had done a lot of different things, it turned out, but the underlying theme was booze. For a few years, then, Dan went back and forth between Ontario and the west coast, living with Joe or Peter or whoever in the east and passing through my or Matt's or whoever's apartment in BC. He seemed to keep himself afloat on student loans—enrolled, technically, at universities in Toronto, Guelph, and Victoria—and claimed to have supportive friends all over. Independent witnesses described him less positively: lots of couch-surfing, nights of crashing in his car, or crashing his car period, ugly drunken scenes, running out on creditors and that fatal aversion to punctuality. He and I had some pleasant reunions and some unpleasant ones—one Christmas night he drove from

Matt's to my apartment, drunk, and became belligerent when I wouldn't serve him any more alcohol. Late on another night, on one of his flash unannounced swings through Vancouver, an acquaintance of us both called me and wearily said, Tell Dan not to come to my place... I have a life. He had acquired a reputation as a bad risk. He was beginning to be written off.

> There were so many friends in Anson's life—scarcely one for whom he had not done some unusual kindness and scarcely one whom he did not occasionally embarrass by his bursts of rough conversation or his habit of getting drunk whenever and however he liked... At twenty-nine Anson's chief concern was his own growing loneliness... Groups of people had a disconcerting tendency to dissolve and disappear. The men from his own college—and it was upon them he had expended the most time and affection—were the most elusive of all. Most of them were drawn deep into domesticity, two were dead, one lived abroad, one was in Hollywood writing continuities for pictures that Anson went faithfully to see.
> —F. Scott Fitzgerald, "The Rich Boy"

Now much of his gentleness had gone, I saw. His good cheer had become a chip on his shoulder, as he lashed out at anyone who dared to say he wasn't a cool guy who was the always-welcome life of every party. Our interesting exchanges about politics or history or literature (Dan was never stupid) were interspersed with his lengthy, self-justifying monologues of how this or that associate had totally let him down or totally sabotaged his good intentions, how he fully meant to get his shit together at last, how he was better or smarter than all those pretentious fucks at university. He would veer from deflecting criticism back at his criticizers, as if pre-empting the censures he secretly knew to be deserved—"He's being completely unreasonable," "They've become really uptight," "I don't know what the fuck *her* problem is"—to offering shameless shows of contrition in lieu of ever actually making amends for himself—"Oh, man, from the very depths of my pitiful soul I once again humbly ask for your forgiveness..." He was now very defensive, speaking a private language of alibis and cajolery. While drinking, he would insist that he had in fact cut back quite a bit, and while missing class he would say how well his courses were going. He talked of Angela often. A note of resentment had crept into his dealings with me—not jealousy, exactly, but snide hints that my stability or my talents as an artist or writer had only come at the expense of my soul and my spontaneity. He was probably right.

We remained friends, of course, but I was rooted, common-law married, and employed, while he kept drifting. My contacts with Dan sometimes made me think of Alan Sillitoe's short story "The Decline and Fall of Frankie Buller," where the narrator acknowledges of his childhood comrade that "there should have been some tree-root of recognition between us, despite the fact that our outer foliage of leaves would have wilted somewhat before each other's differing shade and colour." On New Year's Eve, 1999, we were both in our hometown in northern Ontario once more—I visiting my parents and my in-laws, he sleeping on another guy's sofa—and he came to see me for an hour or so that night. We strolled over to our old elementary school where we'd met, twenty-two years before. I had long since wrung all the nostalgia I could out of the spot, but Dan seemed to find great comfort standing with me under the cold stars in the snow-swept playground, pointing out the sites of childhood triumphs he had never quite been able to surpass: here was where he fought Corey Desjardins and won, the back laneway was where he kissed Tina Sacco, there was where he sneaked his first cigarette. We bade each other Happy New Year, and I politely told him no, it would not be cool for him to drop in at my wife's parents' place. When the millennium turned I was cozy indoors with spouse and family, and Dan was in a bar.

He lived in Toronto for a while with his brother Peter, but a fruitless rendezvous with Angela, a subsequent short-lived romance with another girl, his rejected application to law school and the lingering death of his mother's dog, then in custody of Slime, put him into a steep descent. In 2001 I heard through Joe and Glen that Dan had been incarcerated in a psychiatric ward for a few nights, at the behest of some worried observers, and then I would get rambling wee-hour phone calls from him: turned away by Peter, massively owing for student loans, now sober but chain-smoking and strung out on prescription antidepressants, utterly alone, he was not well. On one of our last meetings I found him hollow-eyed, underweight, and unkempt. He couldn't choose between staying with Joe in Victoria, or Doug, now in Vancouver, or returning to Ontario, and he was restless and listless and somehow frightened—he had confided to me and others of feeling targeted by "an evil force," an alien destroyer undermining his every move. It was as though he'd run out of practical excuses and had to resort to spiritual ones. And he seemed to look to me less as an old friend and more of a potential rescuer, someone to extract a little more sustenance from, a last portion of human warmth or some desperate faint hope. I could not give him much. For several years now he has been in and out of institutions mental and penal, for what may become an indefinite cycle.

It has occurred to me that perhaps all of us who were Dan's friends, and those few who still are, had from the start unconsciously cast him as the inevitable casualty of the circle: when we struggled or stumbled—when Dan himself was there to help— it was taken to be a temporary setback, but when he did, we'd sneer that it was all too typical. Perhaps Dan's decline has thus served as a sacrifice for the rest of us, him deteriorating so everyone else could congratulate themselves and count their blessings that at least they hadn't sunk to his level. Perhaps. But just as probable is the diagnosis of Dan being the victim of his own folly— drink and pride and lack of self-discipline, plus his mother's death and then his obsessive refusal to admit problems or accept blame. I know many who would take that analysis as accurate. Or maybe —slender, speculative possibility—Dan really is right to believe that a demon or devil had found him choice prey, a fundamentally happy and optimistic person who could be dragged through a gauntlet of disappointment and misfortune out of sheer diabolical cruelty, a sick cosmic joke at the expense of our capacity to love and hope and grow wise. I have my doubts, but then many things can happen in twenty-five years and in the end I can offer no earthly accounting for the dark fate of my old friend Dan Tremblay, no sure reasons why it had to be him and no great faith that it was not all foretold in the clouds and the stars and the sky.

Arcadia Borealis

> It's a queer experience to go over a bit of country you haven't seen in twenty years. You remember it in great detail, and you remember it all wrong.
> —George Orwell, *Coming Up for Air*

> There is a town in north Ontario
> With dream comfort memory to spare
> And in my mind, I still need a place to go
> All my changes were there
> —Neil Young, "Helpless"

IN THE EARLY SUMMER of 2003 the Canadian Tourism Commission published a travellers' map of Canada in which all of northern Ontario, bounded by Lake Superior to the south, Manitoba to the west, and Hudson Bay to the north, was mistakenly omitted. There followed an appropriate amount of hell to pay, and dutiful responses from spokespeople and PR flacks defending the region as the nation's "best-kept secret" and insisting that the gaffe would not unduly affect vacationers' holiday plans (in a year when the metropolis of Toronto was crippled by a SARS outbreak and the Alberta beef industry by a mad-cow scare). A foolish error, to be sure, but Northern Ontario has known worse setbacks: this was business as usual in the Canadian Shield.

Among the missing on the defective map was the city where I was born and raised, Sault Ste. Marie. I lived there from 1967 to 1987, often roamed further north of it to Wawa, Thunder Bay, Dryden, and Red Lake, and have gone back intermittently (with longer and longer stretches intervening) in the subsequent years: summer holidays, Thanksgivings, Christmases, weddings, my father's funeral. In 2003, after more than three years' absence, I returned to the Sault (or "the Soo") with my wife and baby daughter, and saw it, perhaps for the first time, as an outsider. It was less a disillusionment than a revelation. In his book *The Day John Met Paul* Jim O'Donnell traced the origins of the Beatles to Liverpool, England, and was surprised to find the Fab Four's roots were, contrary to myth, not in "a rough, tough city of tenement slums and industrial soot... I went looking for a lump of coal; I found a blade of grass." Something similar struck me here.

When I left at age twenty and stopped in at twenty-one or twenty-three or twenty-seven Sault Ste. Marie had been somewhere to leave, but at thirty-six it might have been, of all things, somewhere to live. I wasn't about to relocate myself, but I could see how people could stay where they were. You could study, raise kids, attend galleries, sail, garden, plan, invest, even (if you were fortunate) work there—who knew? It was a gentler, quieter, and more relaxed city than the one I'd emigrated from. With Tonya (herself a Sault native who went away in the mid-80s) and Genevieve (born in New Westminster, BC, six and a half months previously) beside me, I came across detours and developments I'd hardly known in the old days; here were entire mini-worlds in Steelton or the East End or off Great Northern Road where ordinary, adult Saultites were always to be found, this moment or two decades past. When I left, the Sault was crash pads, hangouts, dope connections, and outward-bound trucks rumbling down Highway 17 in the middle of the night, but it had somehow become residences and offices and grocery stores and a diaper run at 9:00 in the morning. We had both changed, I guess.

Like many other communities in northern Ontario, the Sault had made perfect sense in the industrial era of the early twentieth century—with access to minerals for manufacturing, and situated near water for shipping and power generation—but globalization and the Information Age had rendered it less and less viable, geographically and economically. The Sault was now part of Canada's own Rust Belt, as mining, timber, and factory towns across the Maritimes and the higher latitudes of Quebec and Ontario saw their familiar boom-and-bust cycles stall permanently on "bust." That was my recollection of coming to maturity in the north: the gradual understanding that local politicians and businesspeople feared for the city's future with its dependence on the faltering Algoma Steel Corporation, and then my slow perception that, wherever my future lay, it wasn't in Sault Ste. Marie. Most of my peers arrived at the same blunt conclusion. I was never a snob and never pretended to be too talented or too cultured for the Sault and its blue-collar, beer-and-snowmobiles character, but there was no denying that a young person with ambitions of any kind pretty much had to go elsewhere to fulfil them.

That was too bad, because Sault Ste. Marie was not a hick frontier outpost sprung up at the first whiff of windfall. It is, in fact, one of the oldest continuously settled (by aboriginals and Europeans) spots in North America, and its potential and permanence appeared assured with the introduction of strategically vital lock systems on the Canadian and American sides of the St. Mary's River, the steel plant built and expanded under entrepreneurs Francis H. Clergue and Sir James Dunn, and eventually the completion of an international bridge linking the Sault with its Michigan counterpart. Canada's Group of Seven artists' circle had painted many of their best-known works in the surrounding district (e.g. Lawren Harris' *Beaver Swamp, Algoma*, A.Y. Jackson's *First Snow, Algoma*, and Harris' iconic *North Shore, Lake Superior*), when it was at the very edge of the "developed" part of Ontario. The Sault's population had swelled with Italian, Finnish, and Ukrainian immigrants at the turn of the last century and in subsequent decades, and dwellings, schools, stores and services multiplied. Notables from the city ranged from hockey stars Phil and Tony Esposito to realist painter Ken Danby, novelist Frank Paci, and Loonie designer Robert Carmichael. By my 2003 trip many of the streets I wandered and the houses I wandered past were almost one hundred years old: tree-canopied streets of Imperial nomenclature, like Queen, King, Wellington, Brock, Elgin, Simpson, Victoria, Albert, Bishop's Court; three-storey Edwardian and Queen Anne houses of red brick, sturdy verandas, hardwood floors, tidy lawns and gabled roofs. A Sault writer and local hero named Morley Torgov titled his popular hometown memoir *A Good Place to Come From*. It was.

There was another side to Sault Ste. Marie, though, that still coloured my own reminiscence. While in many ways the Sault truly was an attractive small municipality—a travel writer in a *Lonely Planet* guidebook called it "the most appealing of the northern cities," ahead of North Bay, Sudbury, and Thunder Bay—it had always harboured a seedy, shameful underclass. I remember a disproportionate number of flakes and ne'er-do-wells there (a friend encapsulated them as "twenty-five-year-old guys riding dirt bikes") and its remoteness from any other major centre made it a magnet for ill- (or in-) bred backwoods types, hardscrabble farm folk, and poverty- and alcohol-wracked natives. As Algoma Steel began its long decline the welfare rolls increased, and I recall plenty of futile make-work initiatives, rock-bottom rental units, and boarded-up shops. If you rolled in on a Greyhound at 11:30 p.m. the only vehicles on the streets would be cop cars and you could practically see tumbleweeds blowing around. There were violence and crime in the Sault, as well as rough neighbourhoods, bad families, and crooked businesses. And if the city was not so small that everyone knew everyone else, one did hear citywide tales of corruption and cover-ups, whispered stories of "the truth" behind this bigwig's resignation, that administrator's dismissal, or merchant X's bankruptcy. A Sault expatriate I knew recounted a meeting with someone from the Nickel City and saying, "Yeah, Sudbury—the asshole of the world," only to be hit with the rejoinder, "And Sault Ste. Marie—two hundred miles up it." Whenever I told people in Toronto or

Ottawa or Vancouver where I hailed from, there would always be a slightly wary, slightly embarrassed reaction, as if I had survived some legendary disaster or infamous battlefield trauma. The Sault had earned a national reputation no amount of civic boosterism could ever completely negate.

Where was I, then? In the land of my youth, of snow and smokestacks and cargo ships, shared with 80,000 other men and women and children? Or in unfamiliar territory, a backwater of museums and government agencies and the Agawa Canyon tour train, 75,000 inhabitants and shrinking? The Sault had become a personal, private ghost town, still occupied in the everyday sense but abandoned by faces and friends and relations as I had known them. There should be landmarks, everywhere, I felt, hallowed shrines from my life at five or ten or seventeen—where were they? Obscured by newer, later, public attractions: the Canadian Bushplane Heritage Centre (where my dad and I had watched the water-bombers of the Ontario Provincial Air Service rev up for forest fire season), the Roberta Bondar Pavilion (honouring Canada's first female astronaut and alumna of my old elementary school, Alex Muir), the refurbished St. Mary's River boardwalk (my buddies and I used to get high and ponder the vast twilit horizons of the Great Lakes there). In my mind I kept hearing the Pretenders' song, "My City Was Gone," or rereading Thomas Wolfe's epic novel *You Can't Go Home Again*. Tell me about it.

Adults returning to a scene remembered from childhood typically notice how much smaller everything looks, because of course they have grown physically in relation to it. My journey to Sault Ste. Marie in August of 2003 gave me the same awareness, only in terms not of scale but society. It was rather like realizing a favourite playground had really been a weedy parking lot all along, or meeting an influential teacher as a vulnerable, doddering septuagenarian: suddenly the drama or the romance of the memory feels diminished, the whole thing never a big deal to begin with. Since steadily losing population and good name in my day the Sault seemed to have come to terms with itself as a quaint tourist and border town rather than a no-nonsense, productive mill city; now it dawned on me that the Sault had weathered these changes better than I had. The Sault had grown up, but I had grown apart. When I noticed a new warehouse near the train yards I had often walked, my father-in-law explained that it was a storage facility, the only growth industry in a place where so many individuals and families were packing up and moving away. I had contributed to that growth. I was among the exodus, and I was a little hurt to find that Sault Ste. Marie had struggled on without several thousand of its former citizens, including me.

And strolling through my old schoolyards and shortcuts, I had to acknowledge that I was feeling several fading layers of reflection superimposed on each other. I had lived in the Sault long enough to sentimentalize the place when I was still a resident, so in 2003 I could amble by, say, the lot where the house I'd lived in from birth to age eight had stood, and I could remember remembering, as it were: 1975 filtered through 1986, in turn tinted by 1994. Been there, done that, many times over. Much of the sites' emotional resonance had dissipated over the years, leaving a new and chilling melancholy to seep in—the lack of feeling, the flat cold ice of indifference. Revisiting a particular intersection or laneway or storefront once would have meant a welling of spirit and a flood of flashbacks, but now any single one seemed as interesting or uninteresting as whatever was adjacent. Once each setting had signified a discrete point in my growing up and I would have thought, Here was when I was in Grade Four, or Here was when I was in Grade Ten, or Here was when I studied at the School of Hard Knocks, but now I could only think, Here was when I lived in Sault Ste. Marie. It was August, after all, and another frigid Lake Superior winter was on its way. There were no more *frissons* left.

Nevertheless, despite all my reappraisals, in the end there was no final freezing out the primal, ancestral instinct of recognition I still felt in the Sault, however vague, however distant, however dormant within me. I had forgotten many details and confessed to myself that I didn't miss them, yet a deeper and more indelible impression had been retained. It was as though I had never been away, even if I very definitely and very deliberately had. You can't go home again, but home continues to exist, somewhere. Sixteen years later, the worn, not-quite-urban, almost-rural flora and fauna and façades of northern Ontario, the good place to come from and the bad place to admit coming from, had all crystallized for me into one fabled, faraway Arcadia Borealis, my Shangri-La on the Canadian Shield: lost steel plants, lost sidewalks, lost schoolmates, lost sunsets, lost summers, a lost city, a lost self.

The Return of the Native

nostomania—n. Irresistible homesickness; a passion for nostalgia.

An Ojibway Indian, scouting through the forest darkness thousands of years ago, might have come upon it suddenly from a high cliff for the first time— the immense blue glory of Lake Superior. And gazed to the far edge of vision over a scalloped floor of blue, with the tips of thousands of waves pierced by flashing sunlight, like the feet of dancers.
—Al Purdy, *Northern Ontario*

June 14—Burnaby—Golden, British Columbia

Chet Baker, "Imagination," the Eagles, "Lyin' Eyes," Alice Cooper, "Is It My Body," the Rolling Stones, "100 Years Ago"

Driving east out of BC's Lower Mainland on a weekday morning offered as good an illustration as any as to why I was leaving: traffic in my direction was busy but manageable, whereas the westward flow of commuters and transports opposite me was an interminable clog extending from Vancouver through Coquitlam, Pitt Meadows, Surrey, Langley, Aldergrove, Abbotsford, Chilliwack and beyond. For all its prosperity and opportunity, Lotus Land was becoming too crowded, too expensive, too loud, too dangerous, too busy, too *big*. The long crawl of vehicles over and through the suburbs and exurbs and bedroom communities—an all-day, every day mass of metal and smoke and frustration—said it all.

We had been considering the move for some time, sealing our decision with the imminence of our second child and a variety of other family and financial factors. There were the playgrounds where we were the only parents speaking English; the impossibility of ever owning a home like the houses in which we'd grown up, at least not less than two hours out of the city; the urban gauntlet of addicts and panhandlers surrounding my worksite; the irrational but persistent sense of being due, actuarially, to be touched by crime or accident; Genevieve's first Halloween, driving her in a dinosaur costume trick-or-treating between townhouses and high-rise condominiums, sterile and futuristic and ineffably sad. We would miss the jobs and the services and the green spaces and the mild winters, and our friends and co-workers and the handful of other parents and children we had come to know in our neighbourhood, but they were not enough to hold us in the city or the province.

For ten hours I drove, through Hope and up the Coquihalla Highway to Kamloops and Salmon Arm and Revelstoke. A case of a dozen cassettes, favourite albums, mixes, and compilations, was my soundtrack: at certain points the synchronicity between my speed or my view and whatever song was playing sounded like a perfectly scored road movie. I never did see a Sasquatch when I lived in British Columbia, something I always thought I might come across in the thirteen years I lived there, even now beside fast Pacific-bound rivers, ascending the high mountain passes or winding skyward through forest and summit and cloud. The giant primates still kept their distance. I did spot a bald eagle, but I'd seen those even in Burnaby.

BC was a vast land I had never explored much, and my route leaving was only the second time I'd traveled it—the first was when Tonya and I came in on a Greyhound in 1994. Perhaps I had never given it enough of a chance. Then, the bus had been equipped with little TV sets and they showed *The Lion King*, and as we'd ridden down into the Fraser Valley in the sunset I had "Can You Feel the Love Tonight" in my mind, the two of us starting a new life together on the west coast at age twenty-seven, she and I together come what may. Jump ahead thirteen years and the girls, my wife and two BC-born daughters, had already flown out one week prior, so I was left to share the lush alpine scenery that so distinguished the province from the rest of Canada with Max the cat, and he was either snuggled on my lap or cowering underneath my seat. Tired and losing necessary alertness, I pulled into Golden in the crags of the Rocky Mountains. It was all downhill from here. Day One: Me, 1, chipmunks, 0.

June 15—Golden BC—Moose Jaw, Saskatchewan

Gordon Lightfoot, "Did She Mention My Name,"
Merle Haggard, "Silver Wings," Rush, "Subdivisions,"
Ralph Vaughan Williams, *A Pastoral Symphony*

Mountain goats at dawn. Avalanche warnings. Sunrise over the continental peaks of Banff and Lake Louise as Lightfoot sings of Canada. Terrific rainstorm approaching Calgary. Descending down into the foothills of wild rose country. Fuel and food in Strathmore: local Mennonites in traditional garb breakfasting beside natives in nu-metal t-shirts. The prairies spread before me, one hour, two hours, three hours, five hours, eight hours of oceanic grassland—was this how the *Wehrmacht* felt, swallowed up by Russia in 1941? Alberta bound.

Misgivings. I was aware that I might have deluded myself into thinking that I was not only going back geographically but chronologically, to sunny circumstances of my upbringing that just did not obtain anymore. Over the years—even in the last years before I left home—I had perhaps idealized my origins as a Cold War haven of small-town North American tranquility, like Norman Rockwell, or *It's a Wonderful Life*, or Ray Bradbury's *Dandelion Wine*, long-gone dreamlands all autumn and oak trees and innocence. But passing through Medicine Hat and Swift Current I could foresee the truth of what lay ahead: highway cities lined with big-box retail stores and chain hotels, enforcing water restrictions as the pastured centre of the New World dried out in a transforming planet. By Saskatchewan the Trans-Canada highway felt like a rugged dirt road in the badlands. How many more years before the shorebird observatory of Chaplin Lake evaporated? Stopping at last in Moose Jaw and searching for lodgings the foreshadows grew dark. Here was a depleted old downtown, still pleasant in its way but stagnant, fringed with truck routes, strip malls and gas stations. Only two days out of Vancouver and I already missed the cultural diversity. On a walk to get provisions (the place seemed overrun with gophers) I saw only heavyset white people, many grey-haired and most wearing baseball caps, transporting themselves and their offspring Skyler and Brooklynn in SUVs and minivans as they stocked up on nacho chips and Coke. There was more of this in my future.

June 16—Moose Jaw—Kenora, Ontario

> Jimi Hendrix, "If 6 Was 9," Willie Nelson, "Stardust," Tom Waits, "Invitation to the Blues," Harry Connick Jr., "But Not For Me"

Talking to Max and getting no answers. "Almost through Regina, buddy." "Gotta get gas—sit tight, old fellow." "Does this guy think he's going to pass?" "Check it out—crop duster!" Husky restaurant and service stations sell porn magazines, I notice. Trucker essentials, apparently. Place names like Indian Head, Summerberry, Carry the Kettle, Sioux Valley. Through Brandon and Portage La Prairie, Manitoba the trees began to grow again, clusters of maple and birch and poplar on the very rim of the great northern forest. In Brandon in 1994 our Greyhound ride had stopped for evening snacks, and in the restaurant Tonya and I wondered why everyone was transfixed by a big-screen TV that showed a white truck being chased by police down a Los Angeles freeway. Eastward now, the names acquire a French tinge: Fortier, Grande Pointe, Lorette, Dufresne, Ste. Anne. A huge express circuit around Winnipeg and I am approaching the province of my birth. Four down, one to go.

Now I am arrowing into the true Boreal wastes of North America, like Marlow toward the Heart of Darkness. How must the first humans have found it, descendants of Siberian migrants millennia Before Christ—welcome shelter and growth after the barren Arctic, or a limitless pine jungle where bears and wolves and the Wendigo lurked? My route reverses the path of the first Europeans. I am going back through Canada's central breadth of bush and rock that daunted pre-Confederation explorers like Radisson and Groseilliers and Alexander Henry, in a time, Gordon Lightfoot sang, *When the green dark forest was too silent to be real.* Here the signposts read Falcon Lake, Clearwater Bay, Rat Portage, and Keewatin, and the yellow diamond warnings to motorists of moose and deer and fallen rock begin to dot the otherwise empty lengths of two-lane highway. Everything else is water and stone and trees, trees, trees. Dark green and sky blue, dark green and sky blue.

Kenora may be another preview of my ultimate objective. A picturesque waterfront on the idyllic Lake of the Woods, a bush plane base, quiet leafy streets and dignified brick homes—yet empty sidewalks, loitering teens, a staggering drunk and a sense of having barely survived the winter before the meagre warm weeks from mid-June to mid-August. What do people *do* in Kenora? Is there a reason to be here anymore, a local industry to replace forestry or mining or trapping? Do young people hang around for a summer or two waiting tables or cleaning hotel rooms for travellers like me before moving away for good, while the old and the incurious and the solitary hunker down for another five months of snow and isolation? Nice place to visit, but would I want to live there, or anywhere like it? Could I? Could I *again*, if that's really how it is and what I'm really about to do? Day 3: Me, 762, insects, 0.

June 17—Kenora—Thunder Bay, Ontario

> Aerosmith, "Nobody's Fault," Jimmy Cliff, "The Harder They Come," Donovan, "Lalena," Kiss, "Hard Luck Woman"

After Vermilion Bay and into Dryden I am retracing the annual trips I made as a child with my family, when we would go up to Red Lake every summer; thirty-five years later I can't imagine how I endured it as a passenger, since I am barely clinging to consciousness as a driver today. The phrase "the middle of nowhere" must have been coined to depict the infinite kilometres between Ignace and Upsala. This is not the scenic route. What impresses is not the view but the absolute duration of it, only forest and highway, hour upon hour. *The ghastly monotony of wilderness*, complained Aleister Crowley. So mete it be. I speed past a decaying moose carcass, a fresher one later in the morning, stiff and sturdy on the side of the road, and eventually a live specimen, absently grazing in a swamp off to my right. I point it out to Max, who is uninterested. He has moved to the rear window of the little Suzuki, crammed with suitcases and his kitty litter box. The car has become his home. Mine too.

Heading southeast somewhere around English River I see two transport rigs pulled over on the opposite shoulder, their drivers conferring and checking loads. A few minutes up the road there is a trail of debris leading to a car and a camper-trailer stopped on my side where someone flags me down. "Did you see two transports back there?" the young guy asks me as Aerosmith blares out of my window. Yeah, one of them was red. Then I see the camper parked ahead of him has been clipped by the transport, its whole left exterior wall sheared off to reveal a complete cross-section of the inside. At ninety clicks the collision has spaced out the vehicles so that they have come to rest far out of each other's sight, but this is the aftermath: two or three seconds of impact and a highway stretch of wreckage. Whoa. No injuries, though, and the camper operator is calling for help on a cell phone, his vacation ruined but his life spared. Could have been worse. Onward.

Another accident, this one more serious, slows me down an hour or so later. There's an ambulance and police cruisers and another transport, shattered this time. A line of cars comes to a halt and I turn off the engine for a few minutes. Some of the truckers, I notice, are Sikhs, perhaps wondering how they have come so far from the subcontinent only to meet disaster in northern Ontario, a place they probably never imagined before now. They will get to know the region better than they wanted. I'm grateful that my ride is light and therefore fast, making me more manoeuvrable on the highway and less likely to ram or be rammed by another. I've done well so far—no close calls and no empty gas tanks.

In Thunder Bay I stay at my aunt and uncle's, a nice break from the motels. I'm shown old family photographs and mementos, and I'm reminded how deep my roots go in Ontario, and indeed into Algoma itself. Here is my paternal grandfather going off to World War I from Huron County, my grandmother as a girl in Massey maybe a hundred years ago. This was the exclusively Protestant Upper Canada of neat farming and railway towns, and the straitlaced provincial capital of Toronto, where shops closed on Sundays and the Union Jack proudly waved. Those really were different times, visible in the formal poses— even the mugging and laughing youngsters seem somehow more proper and refined than they would generations later—and the images glow with a decency and honour that are not part of our culture anymore. Most of the snapshots were taken outdoors during the day, where the cameras and film of 1914 functioned best, my ancestors and their friends smiling arm-in-arm in a British Empire on which the sun had yet to set. That night Thunder Bay lives up to its name, as a tremendous electrical storm crackles and booms outside, summer lightning strikes echoing off the Sleeping Giant. Max is in the car, safe but no doubt traumatized. Sit tight, old fellow.

June 18—Thunder Bay—Sault Ste. Marie, Ontario

Neil Young, "Birds," ZZ Top, "Francine," Eric Clapton, "Runnin' on Faith," Led Zeppelin, "Rock and Roll"

Grey and rainy outside Thunder Bay. No need to consult the map book anymore. There is just the two-lane Highway 17 to take me through Rossport, Nipigon, Schreiber and further. Fog cuts my speed way down around Terrace Bay, groping and twisting almost blind through ascents and slopes behind campers, trailers, and transports. I see my first "Support Our Troops" bumper sticker while being served coffee and eggs by a pretty waitress at a Husky stop, and I realize that this is the nation's conservative heartland, whose sons and daughters still fight and die on other sides of the world, as alien to them as the bush and snow and civility of northern Ontario would be to a suicidal Afghani tribesman. Going into Marathon I have my first sight of Lake Superior: whitecapped and majestic in the mist, the Big Lake they call Gitchee Gumee. Tonya, Genevieve and Olivia are drinking from this same water. Today I will drink with them.

The highway veers away from the lake after that, and I am in the forest again. Only the car needs fuel now; no more nourishment stops for me. Deep Purple's "Highway Star" roars out of my speakers—it has become my anthem. The Suzuki is thirsty and I have acquired a heavy foot, the gas indicator dropping a little more with every race down a passing lane. Past White River (still "The Coldest Spot in Canada," according to local signs) I finally move to overtake the big rig I have been tailing for an hour, zooming up to 120 while being buffeted by his slipstream. Then another transport is coming up the road right where the three tracks dissolve back to two.

We are aiming straight for each other.

Overdrive. There is no panic, no life flashing before my eyes. Hold her steady. Maintain situational awareness. I make it past my rival and duck back into position just as I run out of lane and buddy, all ten tons of him, lumbers by in the opposite direction. *Hold tight, all right, I'm a Highway Staaarrrrrrrr...*

Should I gas up in Wawa? No, I'm okay. No time to waste. The road is mostly downward here, cutting through ageless rock formations where Dean & Judy sprayed their love in '03; the rocks will endure long after Dean & Judy have worn away. There is the Lake again, flashing briefly in the sun off to my right through gaps between the pine and cliffs, the sand and stones of its empty shoreline like a primordial Baltic or Aegean, touched only by the centuries. The glacial inland sea and the fresh June sky merge on its far horizon. I am steering by instinct now. This is where I come from.

The needle is fluttering on the top bar of "E," flirting with the gauge's orange warning bar. From Wawa to Agawa Bay and Montreal River there are no gas stations, no restaurants, no rest stops, no nothing. I know there's a popular highway store and fuel-up spot around Batchawana Bay, promised by one billboard to be thirty-five kilometres ahead. Fifteen minutes? Twenty?

I eject the cassette; I don't need Metallica's "Seek and Destroy" at this moment. I need gas. I am definitely on E. "The car'll go a long way on E," they always say. I wouldn't worry in traffic-snarled Burnaby, but gunning up and coasting down the unpeopled bluffs of Lake Superior I would. Should I pass this truck and get closer, or hold back and save fuel? Pass by force of habit. Jesus.

That sunk the needle to the middle bar of E, unmistakably married to orange, its flirtation over. Come on, wasn't that thirty-five kilometres already? Will the engine stutter and choke, or just slowly fade to silence? Then there it is, the Canadian Carver souvenir, grocery, and fuel stand. "Twenty dollars' worth of regular, please," I say nonchalantly. Guzzle it up, honey. I even get my windshields cleaned. "Home stretch, buddy," I say to Max, who must know. Next stop: the rest of my life. Seek and destroy.

I am returning to Sault Ste. Marie in pursuit of that vague standard, "quality of life." The city's drawbacks—climate, distance, dearth of jobs, narrower selections of schools, stores, cultural activity and public services—are just outweighed by its advantages—prices, pace, security, family. And if the Sault is no Salt Spring Island, British Columbia or Taos, New Mexico, it does have its own hardy artistic or alternative communities, last vestiges of 60s back-to-the-landers who here eke out modest but satisfying incomes telling fortunes, collecting antiques, exhibiting crafts and organizing folk festivals. Between the economic and social costs of BC's Lower Mainland and the professional and personal sacrifices of the Sault I have chosen the lesser of two evils. It is a gamble that my wife and kids and I are taking in the move, yet I console myself with the words of a colleague at the Vancouver Public Library: "Those whom fate does not lead, it drags," he told me, adding, "Big cities are for young people." Today is my fortieth birthday.

There is much to adjust to. My memories of Sault Ste. Marie, already faint and distorted by twenty years of exile, are due to be painted over by my entry into middle age and the experience of watching my own children grow. We will learn to locate contemporary civic fixtures by the ones from our own day they have replaced, thus: Where's Value Village? K-Mart. Which one's the call centre? Woolco. The new arena? You know, the Memorial Gardens. The seniors' residence? Collegiate High School. I must stop thinking I recognize faces on the street or in the Cambrian

Mall, when I catch myself studying individuals who look dimly familiar to me and then realize they resemble someone I knew not here but in Ottawa or Vancouver—that's how long I've been away. That's how little I recall. Other times I will wonder if the fortysomething moms and dads alongside us at the park or the swimming pool are former neighbours or classmates, someone I loved or hated or fought or befriended or cared for or was cruel to on another plane of reality. The only such unexpected reunion I find is meeting the young couple next door to us on Bishop's Court, who also have two kids of their own. She is a product of Sault Ste. Marie herself, though we never knew her before now, while her husband turns out to be from Red Lake, Ontario. No way.

I have driven 3800 kilometres across the country in five days. I am undergoing the surreal sensation of returning to a home where I have never lived as it currently is, of boldly stepping forward into an unknown remembered past. Things that have long slipped my memory will come back to me, and what I have often looked back on will fade away. The diminutive red Suzuki, jarred by the mountains, dusted by the prairies and washed by the rains of Thunder Bay, can rest for a while; long may you run. I can rest too, for a few hours, before undertaking the remainder of my mortal days in a place where they first began, archiving for an inward chronicle of their course the unearthed shards of mind I have collected in the wider world and which I will still sometimes discover, half-forgotten here and there, in northern Ontario. Lynnwood lives, praise be to Pazuzu, and the Four Freaks will never die.

About the Author

Returned to Sault Ste Marie in 2007 after twenty years away, George Case is a cultural critic and essayist whose well-received previous books have imagined a future history of the world—*Silence Descends: The End of the Information Age* (Arsenal Pulp, 1997), and revealed the story of enigmatic Led Zeppelin legend Jimmy Page—*Magus, Musician, Man* (Hal Leonard, 2007).